"The Object Lessons series ~~i~~ to magic: the books take ordinary—even banal—objects and animate them with a rich history of invention, political struggle, science, and popular mythology. Filled with fascinating details and conveyed in sharp, accessible prose, the books make the everyday world come to life. Be warned: once you've read a few of these, you'll start walking around your house, picking up random objects, and musing aloud: 'I wonder what the story is behind this thing?'"

Steven Johnson, author of *Where Good Ideas Come From* and *How We Got to Now*

"Object Lessons describe themselves as 'short, beautiful books,' and to that, I'll say, amen. . . . If you read enough Object Lessons books, you'll fill your head with plenty of trivia to amaze and annoy your friends and loved ones—caution recommended on pontificating on the objects surrounding you. More importantly, though . . . they inspire us to take a second look at parts of the everyday that we've taken for granted. These are not so much lessons about the objects themselves, but opportunities for self-reflection and storytelling. They remind us that we are surrounded by a wondrous world, as long as we care to look."

John Warner, *The Chicago Tribune*

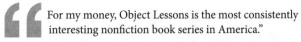

For my money, Object Lessons is the most consistently interesting nonfiction book series in America."

Megan Volpert, *PopMatters*

Besides being beautiful little hand-sized objects themselves, showcasing exceptional writing, the wonder of these books is that they exist at all. . . . Uniformly excellent, engaging, thought-provoking, and informative."

Jennifer Bort Yacovissi, *Washington Independent Review of Books*

. . . edifying and entertaining . . . perfect for slipping in a pocket and pulling out when life is on hold."

Sarah Murdoch, *Toronto Star*

[W]itty, thought-provoking, and poetic. . . . These little books are a page-flipper's dream."

John Timpane, *The Philadelphia Inquirer*

Though short, at roughly 25,000 words apiece, these books are anything but slight."

Marina Benjamin, *New Statesman*

OBJECTLESSONS

A book series about the hidden lives of ordinary things.

Series Editors:

Ian Bogost and Christopher Schaberg

Advisory Board:

Sara Ahmed, Jane Bennett, Jeffrey Jerome Cohen, Johanna Drucker, Raiford Guins, Graham Harman, renée hoogland, Pam Houston, Eileen Joy, Douglas Kahn, Daniel Miller, Esther Milne, Timothy Morton, Kathleen Stewart, Nigel Thrift, Rob Walker, Michele White.

In association with

 Georgia Tech ‖ Center for Media Studies

BOOKS IN THE SERIES

ocean

STEVE MENTZ

Illustrations by Vanessa Daws

BLOOMSBURY ACADEMIC
NEW YORK • LONDON • OXFORD • NEW DELHI • SYDNEY

BLOOMSBURY ACADEMIC
Bloomsbury Publishing Inc
1385 Broadway, New York, NY 10018, USA
50 Bedford Square, London, WC1B 3DP, UK

BLOOMSBURY, BLOOMSBURY ACADEMIC and the Diana logo are
trademarks of Bloomsbury Publishing Plc

First published in the United States of America 2020

Illustrations © Vanessa Daws
Cover design: Alice Marwick

Library of Congress Cataloging-in-Publication Data
Names: Mentz, Steve, author.
Title: Ocean / Steve Mentz.
Description: New York, NY: Bloomsbury Academic, 2020. |
Series: Object lessons | Includes bibliographical references and index.
Identifiers: LCCN 2019037278 (print) | LCCN 2019037279 (ebook) | ISBN 9781501348631
(paperback) | ISBN 9781501348648 (epub) | ISBN 9781501348655 (pdf)
Subjects: LCSH: Ocean. Classification: LCC GC26 .M46 2020 (print) |
LCC GC26 (ebook) | DDC 333.91/64–dc23
LC record available at https://lccn.loc.gov/2019037278
LC ebook record available at https://lccn.loc.gov/2019037279

ISBN: PB: 978-1-5013-4863-1
ePDF: 978-1-5013-4865-5
eBook: 978-1-5013-4864-8

Series: Object Lessons

Typeset by Deanta Global Publishing Services, Chennai, India
Printed and bound in the United States of America

To find out more about our authors and books visit www.bloomsbury.com
and sign up for our newsletters.

for alinor, ian, and olivia

I realized that the sea itself must be the central character whether I wished it or not.

RACHEL CARSON, *UNDER THE SEA-WIND* (1941)*

Shipmates, it is a two-stranded lesson.

**HERMAN MELVILLE, *MOBY-DICK,
OR THE WHALE* (1851)**

CONTENTS

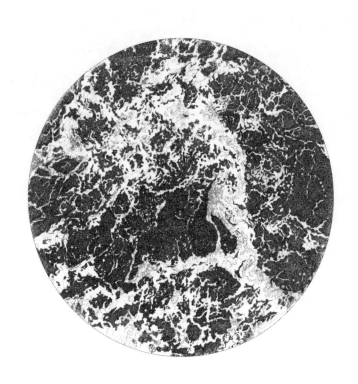

DETERRITORIALIZING PREFACE

Ocean moistens our shared ground. The great waters open up a dynamic environment, fluid, saline, moving, and moved. Our bodies and imaginations register the shift from familiar *terra* to alien *oceanus*. Watery transformation deterritorializes. Radical French theorists Gilles Deleuze and Felix Guattari describe *deterritorialization* as a form of self-emancipation, "the movement by which 'one' leave[s] the territory." Moving offshore reshapes our vocabulary. The ocean needs new words. What happens to "grounded" metaphors when everything solid becomes liquid? Let's start by swapping out the old terrestrial language for saltwater terms.

To move offshore I offer seven words.

Word 1. Current (formerly field): For a long time thinking has happened in fields, areas of expertise imagined to be as stable and reliable as pastures. What if instead we redescribe the adventures of thinking as currents, as rates of flow and change? Why not emphasize movements and connections between or through differences? Fields produce harvests but can lie fallow. Currents flow. We need flow to know Ocean.

Word 2. Water (formerly ground): The thinking that goes by the name "blue humanities" replaces ground, land, and earth as dominant metaphors. Instead we remember that the surface of Earth is mostly Ocean. Our metaphors must float on water rather than resting on ground. In an aqueous environment, nothing stays on the surface forever.

Word 3. Flow (formerly progress): Rethinking movement as flows and circuits rather than progress or retreat can revivify intellectual communities. Thinking in terms of cyclical flows rather than linear progress makes historical narratives messier, more confusing, and less familiar. These are good things.

Word 4. Ship (formerly state): The dissolving force of oceanic history works against nationalism, though at times it may also tend in the directions of global or even imperial totality. Ships, as historians, philosophers, and Hollywood movies have long shown, are symbolic unities, heterotopias, and polyglot fantasy-spaces. Perhaps it is time to imagine politics through ship-to-ship encounters—trading, fighting, hailing, sighting—rather than through the grounded metaphors of the state?

Word 5. Seascape (formerly landscape): This shift seems simple enough as part of the offshore trajectory. But is the "scape" still a problem? Is our language too visual? Underwater creatures seldom rely very much on sight.

Word 6. Distortion (formerly clarity): A basic feature of any aqueous environments is visual distortion. Water bends light. Water-thinking makes distortion a baseline condition. Water's tri-dimensionality sometimes orients us on the buoyant top and at other times closer to the irresistible bottom.

Word 7. Horizon (formerly horizon): Sailors and oceanic historians spend a lot of time thinking about horizons, seamarks, and landmarks. Early modern European sailors heading into the Atlantic spent days looking out for the unmistakable silhouette of Tenerife's volcano, which signaled impending arrival at the Canary Islands, first stop on the transatlantic route. Can horizon be a metaphor for futurity that spans green pastures and blue seas? I imagine horizons as sites of transition, like beaches or coastlines, and also as places where perspectives merge. Horizons of ocean, horizons of currents. These are places from which new things become visible.

This seven-pack of deterritorializing terms can help us think about the blue humanities and break up the Anthropocene.

The blue humanities name an ocean-infused way to reframe our shared cultural history. Breaking up the Anthropocene means reimagining the anthropogenic signatures of today's climactic disasters as a dynamic openings as well as catastrophic ruptures.

These terms make a start. Use them, and we'll change the ocean.

I almost said, "Change the world." But then I changed my words.

1 TWO ORIGINS: ALIEN OR CORE?

Two stories herald Ocean's arrival. In what used to be the most common explanation of the blueness of our planet, Alien water streaked through space on an icy comet that splashed down onto barren rock. In a newer, alternative explanation, Ocean was here all along, its waters stored inside the planetary core of rocky material gathered together billions of years ago when the planet formed. Water, the element that fills up the ocean and makes life possible, either dropped from the sky or oozed out from a solid center. It is Alien, or it is Core. These rival possibilities establish Ocean as an ambiguous thing from its prehistoric origins. It is an object with two meanings, two origins, two stories.

The Alien story describes the radical intrusion of external forces imposing themselves onto a stable, if lifeless, planetary system. Think of that dry rock in the void, four-and-a-half billion years ago, newly created and circling the sun. Onto its jagged surface splashes the ice comet with its Alien cargo. The newly arrived ice melts, spilling across our planet's surface and re-forming our earth as moist and ready for life. So much depends upon this chance encounter in the void, this Alien moisture from above. Space water, while not itself living, creates the conditions without which life cannot begin.

In the Core story no sky-borne messenger appears from on high. Water instead arrives with the rocks that accrete into the planet on which we walk today. In this version of events, the massive impacts and forces that facilitate planetary creation conceal water inside the planet's rocky core, from which depths it seeps up to fill surface basins over geologic time. Ocean need not descend from the sky, but instead the great waters emerge, hidden, from the oldest rocks in our planet's history.

I don't have the expertise to judge the scientific controversy between these opposed stories, but I know why the split matters. These are stories about the origin of Ocean and the blueness of our planet. Without water, and without a planetary temperature range that includes all three of its physical phases—solid ice, liquid water, and gaseous water vapor—life as we recognize it could not have developed on earth. Ocean origins are birth stories. Did we come from the sky or from under the ground? What does it mean that we seem not to be able to choose? Are we Alien or Core?

The story of Ocean's fall from the stars reinforces our terrestrial alienation from the soup of life. We fear the ocean, especially in its stormy moods. Sailors and swimmers know that human bodies can't go there to stay. Ocean surrounds our dry homes as a place of risk, vulnerability, and weakness.

We live near the waters, we employ them, and we love them. But they are not our home.

Unless they are. The Core story, championed by astrophysicist Lindy Elkins-Tanton among others, locates water inside our earth from the start. A leader in space exploration and primary investigator for the planned NASA mission to the metal asteroid Psyche in 2022, Elkins-Tanton has studied the chemical composition of water in asteroids and on earth, and has demonstrated through computer simulations that water can endure the process of planet formation. She describes herself as having become an "evangelist" for "planets getting their water through their common formation processes, and not by later chance." Perhaps, she speculates, more interstellar planets than just ours have formed with watery cores that could support life.

Is our ocean Alien or part of our essential Core? The interlaced stories of how humans have imagined and interacted with the ocean over time show that both contrasting narratives speak lasting truths. Ocean defines our inhospitable home, but even that oxymoron doesn't quite capture the tension and urgency, dependence and fear, in the human-sea relationship. Humans share some evolutionary characteristics with aquatic mammals, including a layer of subcutaneous fat and relative hairlessness. The controversial "aquatic ape hypothesis," in which a crucial phase in the evolution of *homo sapiens* may have occurred in an oceanic or terraqueous environment, remains unverifiable, but it speaks to an "oceanic feeling" that many of us recognize, even if we don't know where it comes from. Herman Melville wasn't an evolutionary biologist or NASA scientist, but the opening chapter of *Moby-Dick* knows what people love: "They must get just as nigh the water as they possibly can without falling in." Poised on the sea's edge, we balance between kinship with and alienation from the watery part of the world. Ocean insinuates its salty fingers into that division and wedges meaning out of both the longing that draws us to the great waters and the fear that drives us away.

I feel both feelings. Every day I walk down the street to a crescent-moon of gritty sand that bears the unoriginal name of "Short Beach." I look out past a pair of rocky headlands onto Long Island Sound. On clear days I glimpse the North Shore of Long Island, about twenty-five miles distant. Sheltered from northeast-churning hurricanes by the massive glacial moraine of the island, my bay in Connecticut is a relatively calm body of water. But like all saltwater inlets it flows into the encircling currents of the World Ocean. Every day in summer and fall, I throw myself into the water's gray-green embrace and think about what it means to put my singular body into the biggest object in the world. It's disorienting and pleasurable and helps me think. According to Diana Nyad, the only person to have swum the hundred miles between Cuba and the United States without a shark cage, swimming creates sensory deprivation and a particular form of physical meditation. Every day I churn sentences through my mind to the rhythm of crawl-stroke arms.

Many of the phrases in the *Ocean* that is this book found me in those salty waters. The meanings of Alien environment and the waters of our Core never strike me more palpably than when I'm swimming, head down, ears and nose clogged, minimally aware. I'm a mismatched terrestrial creature partly at ease in the water, relying on repeated movements of arms and legs to keep me moving and on the surface. I'm also a fleshy bag of water, matching my fluid center to my aquatic surroundings. Both things, always.

What follows elaborates the two stories of the object Ocean. Duality in fact becomes this book's organizing principle; almost everything appears twice. Two accounts describe the planetary origins of seawater. Two myths explain the place of Ocean in Western cultural history. Two poetic voyages engage maritime verse. Two phases of oceanic globalization structure the last half-millennium of human history. Two images of laboring bodies, sailors and swimmers, opposingly define human intimacy with Oceanic forces. Two individual swimmers splash through the final chapter on two different sides of the Atlantic. Throughout, this *Ocean* splashes between the two ways I encounter the great waters, through writing and thinking on the one hand and direct immersion on the other. It's an intellectual project and also a physical practice.

There will be recognizable currents underflowing these pairs of objects and ideas. A tension between solitary swimmers and collectivizing ships will surface throughout. Multiple developments in ocean history will shape this telling, from the dependence of prehistorical communities on the ocean's bounty for sustenance, to sudden bursts of maritime expansion in antiquity and early modernity, to the ambivalent industrial turning-away from the ocean that framed late-twentieth-century Western culture. Oceanic feelings in religious rituals, myths, and psychoanalytic accounts will guide the narrative. Awareness of the controlling force of the "blue ecology" of the ocean, home to roughly 90 percent of our planet's biosphere, will organize my speculations about global warming, ocean acidification, and the ways the ocean floods the center of today's environmental crisis. All these currents reveal Alien and Core influences that flow around us. Human bodies barely touch and only partially know the ocean, even as its waters structure our historical, political, and personal lives.

In what is probably the most influential book written in English about the ocean in the twentieth century, *The Sea Around Us* (1951), Rachel Carson places "that great mother of life, the sea" at the core of the human story. But she also recognizes that when humans touch the great waters, as "in the course of a long ocean voyage," the insights that swim into our imaginations reflect alienation: the sailor "knows the truth that his world is a water world, a planet dominated by its covering mantle of ocean, in which the continents are but transient intrusions of land above the surface of the all-encircling sea." Few sea-writers speak with Carson's particular combination of poetic fervor and scientific exactitude. Her responsiveness to both experience and emotion remains my polar ideal. One way to describe this book might be an effort to juxtapose Carson's precision with Herman Melville's obsessions, but there will be time enough to hurl harpoons after several other deep-diving whales. A different theoretical and historical complement to Carson's material sea appears in the "socially constructed" ocean of geographer Philip Steinberg, who charts the changing political, legal, and economic frames through which humans have understood the ocean. Steinberg writes a complex social history that unfurls the classical Greek geographer Strabo's notion that humans are "amphibious," intimately connected to both land and sea. Bringing together the contrasting strains of Carson's positivism, Melville's mania, and Steinberg's critical theory makes this book intellectually amphibious as well.

These models of ocean thinking do not exhaust even the water's undulating surface, to say nothing of its violet-black depths. Carson's history, Melville's epic, and Steinberg's theory map out entwined planes, but the ocean's verticality plunges down into hidden ways of thinking, including histories of change and human suffering. Another guiding star, to whose work I'll return often, is Martiniquan poet and philosopher Édouard Glissant, who envisions the sea as a site of human crimes and imagined retribution. For Glissant, the essential point of origin is neither Alien arrival nor Core secretion, but instead the drowned human bodies of the Middle Passage whose remains sediment the Atlantic floor. Glissant imagines "the entire ocean, the entire sea gently collapsing in the end into the pleasures of sand, make[s] one vast beginning, but a beginning whose time is marked by those balls and chains gone green." Sunken bodies and rusting chains present a more painful and intimate origin story than comets and planetary accretion. Can a small book have a whale's throat to swallow all these stories whole?

The singularity behind these currents of history and thought is Ocean as object, vast, moving, vibrant, imagined, and ungraspable collective.

Let's dive in.

2 SEAFOOD BEFORE HISTORY

Humans live near water. Water frightens us and lures us into danger, but we never want to be too far from it. Not all the ways in which the words "ocean view" have become the most valuable phrase in the vocabulary of twenty-first-century real estate have deep historical roots—locating fragile and expensive beach houses on barrier islands constitutes a distinctively twentieth-century foolhardiness—but human settlement patterns have always oriented themselves around access to bodies of water. Today, roughly 80 percent of the human population lives within 60 miles of a coast, including freshwater coasts. Freshwater supports agriculture, health, and religious ritual, but saltwater nourishes the imagination. We've needed the sea since prehistory. The bitter waters provide food and transportation. They serve as boundaries and sacred sites. Despite the symbolic appeal of deserts and mountains, there is no human history without the sea.

Theories abound about evolutionary turning points, but the exploitation of marine and tidal resources has a claim to serve as a major inflection point in the 200,000-year story of *homo sapiens*. As maritime historian John Gillis argues in *The Human Shore* (2012), the earliest evidence of human settlement, at Pinnacle Point, South Africa, suggests that access to maritime resources, including fatty acids in fish and shellfish, helped support an increase in brain development before humans first left Africa 50,000 years ago. Armed with larger brains, *homo sapiens* went on to settle the globe, displacing other early species of genus *homo* such as the Neanderthals, and hunting megafauna largely to extinction. Gillis summarizes recent work by archaeologists, anthropologists, and neurochemists to claim that "it was only when humankind reached the sea that the brain could evolve to its present human dimensions." What Gillis calls humankind's "journey to the shore" started in the African savannah where our species first appeared, but the evolutionary changes wrought by the rich foods of tidal ecotones drove crucial brain developments. Only dolphins and other marine mammals, who have direct access to marine foods, match the brain-to-body ratio of *homo sapiens*. The big brains of humans, which Gillis describes as "our distinguishing trait," may have formed first through contact with the sea. The sea was certainly not the only factor in the evolutionary path that forged *homo sapiens,* but proximity to its bounty may have been crucial in the development of modern humans.

This coastal theory of brain development presents a nutritional and cultural reinvention of the "aquatic ape" hypothesis. First proposed by Alistair Hardy in 1960 and expanded by feminist scholar Elaine Morgan in the 1970s and 1980s, the hypothesis that humans evolved at least partially in an aqueous environment remains controversial. The timescale needed for substantial evolutionary changes in species development seems not to be met by the coastal environments for which we have prehistoric evidence of human settlement. The expansion of multiple species of genus *homo* around the world also mitigates against the strongly Darwinian argument that Hardy and Morgan put forward in their different ways. But the theory that early humans relied on coastal subsistence for many millennia before and during the global expansion of *homo sapiens* remains actively under exploration by scholars of prehistory and evolutionary biology.

Early histories of human culture often center around either the development of agriculture in the Fertile Crescent around 12,000 years ago, or the 20,000-40,000-year-old Paleolithic cave paintings found from Europe to Indonesia. Both these origin stories discount the amphibious tale that Gillis relates in which "shores were humankind's first Eden." With the exception of rare sites such as Pinnacle Point, much of the archaeological evidence of early human coastal dwellings likely sits under 250–300 feet of sea-level rise since the end of the last ice age, roughly 12,000 years ago. If the theory of coastal settlement and changes in brain development around 50,000 years ago is correct, evidence of this amphibious explosion of human physical and cultural evolution mostly lies on the floors of coastal seas. The movement of *homo sapiens* out of Africa to settle the Fertile Crescent, Asia, Europe and Australia, and the Americas would not have meant abandoning the sea but rather moving along what archaeologists term the "the Kelp Highway" into new coastal ecotones that were ripe for amphibious gathering. When the land bridge connected Siberia to Alaska, early human groups appear to have followed the shoreline into the Americas, harvesting shellfish as they went. The hunting of large mammals that would lead to the extinction of mammoths and many other species may be considered a supplement to this coastal foraging, or perhaps a survival skill developed by humans in areas such as central Europe that lacked sufficient coastal resources for a growing population.

Considering the seacoast as preagricultural Eden means displacing the pastoral garden from the center of our cultural imagination. The Hebrew scriptures, written during the so-called Axial Age when large-scale agricultural civilizations were developing religious traditions throughout Asia and the Near East, exclude the sea from Paradise. Ocean voyaging signaled divine punishment for Noah and Jonah, and laboring in fields represented both the punishment for disobeying God's command in Eden and also the return to the land after the Flood waters receded. In the Christian Book of Revelation, the post-apocalyptic arrival of "a new heaven and a new earth" comes through universal drying-out of ocean water: "there will be no more sea" (Rev 21:1). As the cultural geographer Christopher Connery has noted, the turn against the sea in Revelation parallels a common Near Eastern mythic structure in which a male god of the earth defeats a female divine embodiment of the ocean. The feminist Christian theologian Catherine Keller has suggested that the text of Genesis, in which God's spirit moves "over the surface of the deep" (Gen 1:1), indicates the nascent presence of tehomic or oceanic divinity. Joining Keller's theology to Gillis' prehistory, we might speculate that the ancient divinity seen fitfully and fearfully in the great waters echoes our species' ancient connection to coastal ecotones. Agricultural civilizations, in this reading, turned their collective backs on the sea.

But in the pre-apocalyptic world of human history, the sea has always been alien but never absent. Even in prehistory, sea travel and maritime exchange, as well as river-based trade, were essential to human thriving. Archeologist Barry Cunliffe argues that Europe's geographical position facing Atlantic, Mediterranean, and Black Sea coastlines, "between the oceans," structured its cultural and physical expansions over the past 11,000 years. Human proximity to the sea has also underwritten water's symbolic presence in religion and artistic cultures. The religious meanings of the ocean include profundity as well as hostility. In Hebrew scriptures, when Jonah descends into the whale's belly, he encounters the divine truths that the Psalmist believes that sailors also see: "They that go down to the sea in ships, that do business in great waters; / These see the works of the Lord, and his wonders in the deep" (Psalm 107). Contemporary scientist and activist Wallace J. Nichols' notion of "blue mind" suggests ways in which the human fascination with the sea undergirds medical sciences, psychology, and water sports. Thinking more broadly about the religious meanings attributed to the sea in many cultures, historian of religion Kimberly Patton explores the sea as a vehicle for purification on both individual and global levels. Taking her mantra from Euripides, "The sea can wash away all evils of humankind" (*Iphigenia at Tauris*), Patton sees the modern history of the ocean as a painful overlap between "the exigencies of religious purity and human habits of waste disposal." As industrial waste has fouled the great waters and the oceans have acidified due to their uptake of carbon, ancient beliefs about the sea's infinite vastness collide with tangible evidence of degradation. Patton describes a "paradox . . . in contemporary attitudes toward the sea that strangely mingle awestruck love with relentless abuse." Both the love and the abuse ring true—but neither can extend itself forever.

The sea-love that Wallace Nichols finds in California surf culture echoes the sea-harvesting that supported early populations of coastal *homo sapiens* 50,000 years ago. In both cases an alien environment supports and lures. Through direct and indirect contact with the sea, its resources, its coasts, and its physical being, humans have always defined themselves in dialogue with alien and inhospitable waters. The "blue mind" evangelism that Nichols trumpets—sea-bathing for him is both medicine and therapy, as it also was for the early-nineteenth-century doctors who treated supposedly "hysterical" women with forced cold-water dunking—bridges the gap between Ocean/Blue and Human/Mind. Nichols believes in Ocean as a biological, historical, and evolutionary source to which we can return. The key task today for sea-thinkers like him, Patton, and environmentalist Carl Safina is to learn to see the sea. The alien ocean must come fully into view. To create what Safina calls a "sea ethic," a marine companion to Aldo Leopold's famous "land ethic," requires imaginative engagements with alien spaces. "The sea demands a reckoning," says Kimberly Patton. Blue reckoning requires that we look back into the human past as well as forward into the ocean's perilous present and future.

The ancient humans who followed the Kelp Highway out of Africa around the globe were unlikely to have been superheroic swimmers along the lines of Lynne Cox or Michael Phelps. As coastal foragers and denizens of the fertile ecotone where sea meets land, they may well have been more routinely aquatic that their urban and agricultural descendants, but even the "aquatic ape" hypothesis does not claim that early humans were marine mammals. Rather, the particular qualities of early human societies, from brain size to tool-making, appear to have co-evolved with the watery part of what Herman Melville trumpets as "this terraqueous globe." The past century has seen a massive turn, especially among wealthy Westerners, toward blue water as a marker of aesthetic value and a site of recreation. In Nichols' estimation, globally "more than 500 million people choose water-based recreation as a means of exercise, escape, challenge, relaxation, excitement, and play"—a number that he notes would be much higher if it added the millions more who use water in religious rituals. John Gillis argues that, as twenty-first-century human populations become less tied to agricultural labor, the terrestrial myth of Eden as a landlocked garden not only "misrepresent[s] our past but now, when for the first time more humans live in cities than on the land, it is wholly misleading about our future." The nutritional value of seafood before history stimulated early human brains and sounds a blue echo that is now pinging in our ears. To follow surf culture into the waves might not simply be acceding to another California trend. Instead, engaging with the blue makes visible the alien environment that has splashed alongside human physical and cultural evolution throughout history. As Amitav Ghosh observes in *The Great Derangement* (2016), the great urban centers founded during the colonial age of maritime empires, including New York, Mumbai, Miami, Singapore, and Sydney, cluster at the seacoast, where they are vulnerable to rising sea levels and storm surge. Responding from these cities to today's environmental conditions requires that we re-engage with the sea in our lives, our politics, our cultures, and our urban planning.

Many historians who consider the role of land and sea across the long span of human history have described sudden turns toward or away from the sea. The example of Ming China's destruction of its massive oceangoing fleet in 1525, not long after the voyages of Zeng He had traversed the

Indian Ocean to the east coast of Africa, represents a specific and radical shift of the sort that historical thinkers are eager to find. The Nazi jurist Carl Schmitt, in his meta-historical volume *Land and Sea* (1954), interprets world history as a series of "spatial revolutions." For Schmitt, writing in the early 1950s as the postwar European and global order was coming into shape, the most important spatial revolution in human history was the oceanic turn of the European powers after Columbus, which he calls "the first complete space revolution on a planetary scale." Similarly, but from the poetic left, Charles Olson claims in *Call Me Ishmael* (1947) that Melville's turn toward the Pacific represents the "third and final Odyssey" and that "America completes her West only on the coast of Asia." These and other visions of maritime empires surge far away from small groups of prehistoric humans gathering shellfish and kelp in tidal pools. But they share with French philosopher Gaston Bachelard the conviction that "the true eye of the earth is water." The ocean in these polyglot intellectual currents represents blue Core and Alien heart. Humans live near the ocean, play in it and pray in it, and live off its ecological bounty. But we never comprehend it.

3 MYTH I: ODYSSEUS, NOT ACHILLES

The man weeps, staring out at the waves and longing for home.
The godlike boy rages and clogs the river with the corpses of his enemies.
Which hero is our hero?

The philosopher Michel Serres observes that when Achilles fights against the river in Book 21 of Homer's *Iliad*, the struggle allegorizes human violence against Nature. The superhuman warrior, as a byproduct of his assault on his Trojan rival Hector, fills the water with blood, mud, and corpses. The river-god Scamander splashes to his own defense, and the inhuman waters threaten even the mightiest of the Achaeans. The battle that ensues matches man against god, mortal body against flowing current. Christopher Logue's twenty-first century free translation captures the scene's violence:

> Picking his knees up, Achilles, now
> Punting aside a deadman, now swimming a stroke or two,

Remembered God's best word and struck
Like a mad thing at the river. He beat it
With the palm of his free hand, sliced at it,
At the whorled ligaments of water, yes, sliced at them,
Ah!—

Can the warrior slice water? Will River defeat the hero? Perhaps the ability to injure the landscape is the epic hero's primal talent, the end point of his godlike excess and lust for victory. To the extent that murderous and doomed Achilles sits at the center of Western heroism, this episode, as Serres emphasizes, captures the hostility between Man and Nature. River is not quite Ocean, but Achilles' struggle against Scamander represents a basic environmental hostility. Alien fluid threatens the human hero. Water may be able to drown his singular body, even this godlike man, "best of the Achaeans":

And the water's diamond head
Shut over Achilles, locked round his waist
Film after film of sopping froth, then
Heaved him sideways up while multitudinous crests
Blubbed around his face, blocking his nostrils with the
    blood
He shed an hour before.

The translator's adjective "multitudinous" echoes Macbeth's description of "multitudinous seas," giving the English passage about the river an oceanic flavor. Scamander's water tastes salt from Achilles' blood, as well as the blood of the innumerable Trojan corpses damming up its current. Violence, including the divine rage against Troy that undergirds Achilles' quest for Hector, reds the clear stream. As Serres shows, this side-battle that distracts the hero in the war for Troy represents the human destruction of nonhuman environs that has fouled the waters of our blue planet from antiquity through today. Homer's solution to the impasse, put into operation by "Hera, Heaven's queen," counters Scamander's water with divine fire. Hephaestus burns back the raging waters so that the field clears for Greeks to butcher Trojans. Chastened, the river-god returns to his course: "between his echoing banks / Scamander / Rushed gentled over his accustomed way." In the war epic, killing humans remains the central focus. Achilles' tussle with Scamander represents a side-turning in the battle for Troy. But the heroic image that the warrior creates, in which the need for victory overrides any environmental destruction it creates, has long-term resonance, up to and including the present day. What is global warming but a planet-sized battle waged by humanity against the world-girdling river, Oceanus?

Odysseus fights alongside Achilles at Troy, but his crafty heroism engages with fluid environments very differently. Tears, not rage, frame his encounter with Ocean. The *Odyssey* opens by describing "the man" with the famously untranslatable epithet *polytropos*—trickster, a man of many turns and tropes, "a complicated man," in Emily Wilson's recent version. When the epic picks up Odysseus' story, he sits facing the ocean, weeping his inability to perform the bloody combat into which Achilles heedlessly plunges. The goddess Calypso tries but cannot comfort him:

> She found him on the shore. His eyes were always
> tearful: he wept sweet life away, in longing
> to go back home . . . [/]
> > By day he sat
> Out on the rocky beach, in tears and grief,
> Staring in heartbreak at the fruitless sea.

The complicated man longs in sadness for the alien element. At this point, he's a sailor not a fighter. The sea engages Odysseus more directly than the river does Achilles. In the *Iliad*, the godlike warrior's struggle against the water distracts him from his mad rush toward Hector. But in the less direct turnings of the *Odyssey*, the ocean presents itself as both barrier and road. The man must sail through waves and shipwreck into them. "Let this come too," he tells Calypso when she releases him to sail home.

The hero of craft not wrath builds his own boat, with the goddess's help, but the shipwreck that follows requires not just skill and strength but also his ability to orchestrate multiple forces in an aquatic environment. The craft he fashions with Calypso's help splits under the force of Poseidon's storm. Unwilling to abandon even its fragments, he at first refuses the advice of the sea nymph Ino, who instructs him "With just your arms / swim to Phaeacia." Odysseus the mariner seeks multiple allies in his "sea of sufferings" and "odyssey of pain." He waits until "the waves have smashed my raft to pieces" before he turns to swimming, though when he plunges into the rough waters he does not neglect Ino's token:

> He took off the clothes
> Calypso gave him, but he tied the scarf
> around his chest, and dove into the sea
> spreading his arms to swim.

Surviving at sea requires careful accounting; only after having exhausted the support of his first goddess-ally, Calypso, does Odysseus turn to Ino's scarf and swimming. The poet imagines swimming as a composite act, mutually performed by the magic of the goddess and the hero's skilled arms. After two days and nights of swimming, his arrival on Phaeacia requires another human and divine collaboration. Faced with sheer cliffs and violent surf, Odysseus steers himself toward the mouth of a river where his dual strategy combines strong swimming with supplication to the river-god. The tactics work together. A river-god like the one against which Achilles fought at Troy welcomes sea-strained Odysseus to shore:

> The current ceased; the River God restrained
> the waves and made them calm. He brought him safe
> into the river mouth. His legs cramped up;
> the sea had broken him. His swollen body
> gushed brine from mouth and nostrils.

These two episodes, in which Achilles fights one river and another river saves Odysseus, call to each other across the expanse of Homer's two epics. They show two inversely mirrored forms of heroism. The godlike warrior, doomed to die at Troy, spills his wrath into Scamander's flood in ways that prefigure how human industry has despoiled our planet. The crafty man, by contrast, finds help from a sympathetic freshwater river, whose powers reach into the salt surf to succor him. The moment in which Odysseus makes landfall finds the hero, tormented by sea-suffering, crawling under "two dense bushes growing together" to sleep. Once again, his tactical acumen in choosing dense foliage for shelter works in concert with the divine aid of his patron Athena, who "poured down sleep to shut his eyes / so all his painful weariness could end." Having escaped the sea, the man rests. He will never muster Achilles' god-fighting rage, but in its place he proffers maritime balance and a combination of tactics, tools, and endurance. He is sea-hero and assembler of complex technologies. The man loves and fears the Ocean—like so many of us today.

Literary scholar Northrup Frye once quipped that "all critics are either *Iliad* critics or *Odyssey* critics." Like Frye, I fall on to the *Odyssey* side of the scale, but for slightly different reasons. I too am somewhat uncomfortable with the venerable tradition that lauds "seriousness," warfare, rage, and the violent childishness of Achilles outside the walls of Troy. I recognize what Frye calls "tragedy, realism, and irony" as markers of high value, but I'm not sure that the wrath of Achilles, and the lineage of male tragic whiners who descend from Achilles, including Oedipus, Hamlet, Ahab, and Ralph Ellison's Invisible Man, exhaust the fullness of human experience. These heroes of rage and struggle represent godlike grandeur, but they also pollute the human and nonhuman environments they inhabit. Who wants to inherit Thebes or Denmark or even Ellison's New York after these heroes have broken their kingdoms? We admire these figures, and we learn things from them. But they produce more problems than solutions.

Turning to the *Odyssey* side of the equation does not only mean, as Frye claims, embracing "delight." My defense of Odysseus as heroic model does not rely, as Frye's does, only on redemptive ideas about pleasure, indirection, or trickery. Instead, I'm an Odyssey-critic because I'm an Ocean-critic— not to mention a saltwater swimmer. Odysseus models the ambivalent encounter between marine vastness and human particularity. To engage Ocean as object means sailing and swimming with Odysseus.

I'll end this chapter with five ways in which Odysseus points toward Oceanic heroism and an intimate if vexed relationship between humans and the sea.

The hero as boat-builder: Odysseus invents, designs, and manufactures his own tools, from the wooden spear he sharpens to blind the Cyclops to the "I am Nobody" pun with which he taunts the monster. He epitomizes *homo faber*, the human builder who uses designed materials to compensate for the relative weakness of his body. He crafts with his own hands both the wooden bed that symbolizes his marriage to Penelope and the wooden boat in which he leaves Calypso's island.

The hero as meteorologist: In addition to his mechanical technologies, Odysseus knows how to decipher supernatural weather. All Greek heroes recognize that they depend upon divine favor, but while Achilles ends up fighting the river-god, Odysseus shrewdly milks his favor with Athena, Ino, and Calypso to support his long journey home. He learns to read the weather, even if that requires that he learn to placate jealous goddesses.

The hero as trickster: Odysseus fights and kills his enemies, and his story includes both the heartless slaughter of the suitors at the epic's end and the reckless sacking of the innocent city of the Cicones soon after he departs ravaged Troy. But his particular strain of heroic skill owes less to martial directness than to a mixing of multiple techniques. He strategizes, uses tools, and depends on the extrahuman forces of wind and tide. Words may be his most powerful tool, but he's also good with a tiller, a bow, or a hand-fired spear.

The hero as sailor: When the river surrounds Achilles he lashes out. When Odysseus' boat wrecks beneath him, he swims—after first constructing a virtual second boat out of Ino's scarf. Even when plunged into the hostile element, Odysseus nevertheless is never quite naked: he has allies, tools, divine patrons around him at all time. He's always sailing something.

The hero as swimmer: As industrial modernity switched from sail to steam and later to diesel, and as commercial airplanes have replaced long haul sailing as the most common way to travel the globe, the iconic figure of the working sailor has receded from cultural prominence. The rise of recreational swimming in both freshwater and saltwater, and after the mid-nineteenth century in purpose-built pools, has come to displace the sailor in cultural practice. Odysseus, who idealizes the human relationship with Ocean, represents both sailor and swimmer—though making his example speak to the twenty-first century's more immersive vision requires some interpretive ingenuity.

Odysseus' literary and cultural genealogy is long and varied, including versions of Ulysses in Shakespeare and James Joyce and variations on the theme in literary protagonists from the salty, such as Melville's Ishmael and Conrad's Lord Jim, to the landlocked, such as Jane Austen's Lizzy Bennett and George Eliot's Dorothea Brooke. The protagonist who triumphs by wit and skill, by rhetoric and persuasion, occupies the Odyssean position in Western literature. Taking Odysseus as keystone emphasizes this tradition's roots in craft, including, but not limited to, maritime skills. The man who weeps on the beach, sails into the storm, and swims to shore represents our most Oceanic hero.

4 WET GLOBALIZATION I: THE PREMODERN ANTHROPOCENE

When the supercontinent Pangea fractured and began to drift into distinct continents 750 million years ago, the ecosystems of the newly separated land masses began to diverge from one another. Only limited contact ensued between the massive land mass on which humans first evolved, Afro-Eurasia, and the distant ecosystems of the Americas. During the most recent ice age, which ended around 12,000 years ago, water levels were low enough that many animals, including humans, traveled across the land bridge connecting Siberia to North America. But after the ice melted and the seas rose, the separation of the ecospheres became closer to absolute. Birds crossed the oceans, a small number of Viking ships crossed the North Atlantic around 1000 CE, and the range of maritime exploration of Pacific Island cultures remains difficult to discern precisely. But in broad terms, the living networks and human ecologies of the Americas remained separate from those of the larger connected landmass of Afro-Eurasia between the dawn of history and the late fifteenth century CE. During many thousands of years, animal, plant, viral, and human ecologies on each side of the Atlantic and Pacific basins developed in isolation from each other. The overfamiliar date of 1492 fingers Columbus at the start of a new era of ecological globalization, but the arrival of the Portuguese fleet led by Vasco da Gama in India in 1499 demonstrates that the rapidly developing global maritime network of trade, violence, colonization, and empire also faced east. In the phrase of earth systems scientists Simon Lewis and Mark Maslin, the era that scholars call the "early modern" period witnessed the creation of a "New Pangea" that relinked the ecologies and economies of once-sundered continents.

Many different names have been proposed for the period in which European sailors took to the World Ocean, encircled the planet, and began to occupy the global spaces of world history. The environmental historian Alfred Crosby influentially proposed the term "Columbian Exchange" in 1972, inaugurating a tradition that would treat Columbus' voyages to the Americas as the essential first steps in global transformation. Crosby's focus, however, was on an ecological process not an individual. He focused on the physical interweaving of the living and nonliving networks of the sundered parts of Pangea. Bringing these ecosystems back together, he observed, pushed unlike systems into becoming increasing like each other. "That trend toward biological homogeneity," Crosby writes, "is one of the most important aspects of the history of life on this planet since the retreat of the continental glaciers." Charles C. Mann's two works of global ecohistory, *1491: New Revelations of the Americas before Columbus* (2005) and *1493: Uncovering the New World Columbus Created* (2011), have done much to communicate the consequences of Crosby's vision. Mann emphasizes the "role of *exchange*, both ecological and economic" in what was "not . . . the discovery of a New World, but its creation." Marxist ecohistorian Jason W. Moore points out that the development of frontier capitalism during the early modern period gave rise to a "world-ecology" of appropriation and exploitation. "Capitalism," Moore argues, during this era became "a way of organizing nature" on a global scale. Historians of the period between 1400–1800 CE also use categories like "early modernity," and the older Eurocentric term "Renaissance," to describe a process of cultural expansion that can also be accurately named "globalization." An older historical tradition refers in Eurocentric terms to the "discovery of the oceans" after the fifteenth-century voyages to Asia and the New World. In an almost certainly vain effort to avoid canonizing individuals, I suggest that we ignore Columbus and instead describe this period as "wet globalization," because its crucial technology was the oceangoing ship and its anti-fundamental environment the sea.

In describing "wet globalization," I like to use the phrase "offshore trajectory" because those words emphasize that oceanic expansion relies upon global movements on and of saltwater. Sea travel connected humans, nations, empires, and religions—not to mention plants, animals, viruses, and ecosystems. Globalization operates now and has always operated through sea routes, from the Spanish silver trade that linked the Pacific coast of the Americas to the Philippines to China in the sixteenth century through efforts underway in the summer of 2018 by Russian ships to open the Northwest and Northeast Passages through no-longer-icebound Arctic waters. Even though today most individuals, at least most relatively wealthy individuals, travel the globe by air, the goods that comprise the global economy still travel by ship. Shifting our attention from firm ground to the unstable fluid covering most of our planet's surface emphasizes that many events in the so-called Age of Discovery emerged through forces and encounters that were largely beyond the control of individual humans. The well-known figures who have been canonized as "discoverers" or "explorers" were not in control of their voyages. It may be too late at this point to rename the "Columbian Exchange" with less focus on one man, though one of my arguments for "wet globalization" is the way the phrase captures the impersonal nature of the forces at work during this period. The World Ocean, with its interwoven patterns of currents and prevailing winds, drove the populations of the separated continents back together. No single mariner, nation, or community fueled those voyages by themselves. The New Pangea floats on the sea.

For Lewis and Maslin, in their earth systems science perspective, wet globalization in the early modern period marks a new phase in anthropogenic climate change. This period, they argue, fixes the origins of the modern world ecosystem. In nominating the year 1610 as the "Orbis Spike," their proposed "Golden Spike" marker inaugurating the Anthropocene, they emphasize the more-than-human consequences of this moment in human history:

In Earth systems terms it is the last globally cool moment before the long-term warmth of the Anthropocene, and the key moment after which Earth's biota becomes progressively globally homogenized . . . thereby setting Earth on a new evolutionary trajectory.

The scientists choose 1610 as an observed minimum for carbon levels after the substantial depopulation and subsequent afforestation of the Americas. Carbon output would later increase rapidly after industrialization and global population growth up to and through the present day. While, as a humanities scholar who believes in stories, I remain suspicious of all magic numbers, their nomination of 1610 makes a valuable contrast to Columbus' 1492. For Lewis and Maslin, the Age of Man begins as an Age of Death: historical analysis of the death rate of Native American populations estimate that at least 70 percent of the precontact population, and perhaps as high as 90 percent, died within the first 150 years after the arrival of Europeans and the viruses that sailed with them.

Total human casualties during the period of contact and early colonization range from 50–76 million. European settlers planted their flags on depopulated American continents. "The arrival of Europeans in America," Lewis and Maslin write, "probably killed about 10 per cent of all humans on the planet over the period 1493 to 1650." The decimation of the Americas in the early modern period holds up a horrific mirror in which we can glimpse worst-case scenarios of large-scale climactic disruption today. The bleak visions that David Wallace-Wells describes in *The Uninhabitable Earth* (2019) approach, at their worst, the destruction wrought on the indigenous cultures of the Americas during the early modern period. Lewis and Maslin show that the key underlying technology that dramatically reshaped our environment on a planetary scale was long haul transoceanic shipping:

> The 1610 Orbis Spike marks the beginning of today's globally interconnected economy and ecology, which set Earth on a new evolutionary trajectory. [. . .] In narrative terms, the Anthropocene began with widespread colonialism and slavery: it is a story of how people treat the environment and how people treat each other.

The World Ocean flowed with the blood of Native Americans in the years after contact. Soon after the drowned bodies of the Middle Passage would further stain the waters.

From the red waters of conquest, slavery, and settlement emerged the new ecological order of globalization. The material and symbolic centrality of two genocides—the disease-plus-colonialism-driven extermination of Native Americans, and the brutal displacement of the transatlantic slave trade—places early modernity's crimes in oceanic context. The key technology for both forms of oceanic globalization was the sailing ship. In his autobiography of being captured and sold into slavery, *The Interesting Narrative* (1789), Olaudah Equiano emphasizes his shock when he first saw "the sea, and a slave ship," which things "filled me with astonishment, which was soon converted into terror, which I am yet at a loss to describe." Seeing in the ship and its festering hold the monstrosity that would rupture his life, Equiano faints. Many years later he writes his way into partial understanding. Édouard Glissant would expand upon Equiano's vision by claiming that the slave ship and the Caribbean waters into which African bodies were thrown capture the hard birth of something new in the world:

> This boat is your womb, a matrix, and yet it expels you. This boat: pregnant with as many dead as living under sentence of death.

The multiplicity that Glissant names *Relation* launches itself out from the womb of the Middle Passage. Historian Marcus Rediker argues in his award-winning *The Slave Ship: A Human History* (2007) that oceangoing ships transporting human cargo from Africa to the New World shaped global modernity. The living and dead with whom the ships were "pregnant," in Glissant's term, formed the crucible of the global economy and ecology that would define the modern era. Rediker cites W. E .B. DuBois' observation that the slave trade was the "most magnificent drama in the last thousand years of human history." Rediker shows in detail how that tragic drama relied on the historical practice of transoceanic navigation. The history of the Middle Passage, Rediker concludes, contains as its heart the inchoate "terror" experienced below decks of the slave ship. Around that ship, managing its buoyancy and its direction, a maritime culture steered the world into a new phase of globalization. "The sea is history," intones the sonorous verse of Caribbean Nobel Laureate Derek Walcott. But also, counters British-Guyanese writer Fred D'Aguiar, "The sea is slavery." Both poet and novelist recognize that Ocean traces the fluid connections between history and slavery.

Any consideration of early modern wet globalization guides our attention inevitably toward the slave trade, as if drawn gravitationally by forces of cruelty and world-changing evil. The devastation and upheaval wrought by nonhuman agents during wet globalization, in particular the Afro-Eurasian diseases that devastated Native American humans whose bodies lacked antibodies to counter them, may have killed a larger number than did the slave trade—but the moral blindness of slaver and settler alike exposes the fundamental inhumanity that was the harbinger of early globalization. As Lewis and Maslin observe, the choice of any hinge-point in the long arc of ecological history leading to the Anthropocene amounts to a narrative choice. Their choice of 1610 and the wet ecological globalization that brought forth the violent birth of the New Pangea emphasizes human cruelty as well as unintended ecological consequences as drivers of climate change. On a physical level, global catastrophe emerged from the saltwater substrate on which violence floated, across which viruses and bacteria traveled to the New World, by means of which the separated ecosystems re-merged into a single global system.

The devastating consequences of wet globalization for the New World included the collapse of major Native American polities in Mexico, Peru, and elsewhere. The societies that arose in the Americas, both as European colonies and as independent nations, developed as ocean-centric states. Maritime passages to and from Europe and Asia dominated the trade in goods such as sugar, rum, tobacco, and indigo, as well as the transoceanic traffic in slaves. The cultural consequences of living inside this global system include a particular obsession with human liberty. As American historian Edmund Morgan has observed, "the growth of freedom experienced in the American Revolution depended more than we would like to admit on the enslavement of more than twenty percent of us at that time." Morgan emphasizes not just the material contributions of enforced labor—the slaves that built the White House—but also the ideological gymnastics required to justify a slave-holding nation that was dedicated to human liberty. The presence of enslaved people germinated an exaggerated and hypocritical ideology of freedom that still pervades the hybrid cultures of the New World.

The omnipresence of maritime slavery in the early modern Americas also generated a distinctive freedom-story known as *marronage*. The fantasy of escaping from slavery to build a free society became historical fact in many locations. Maroon communities of escaped slaves included such disparate groups as the *cimarones* in Panama, with whom Sir Francis Drake made an anti-Spanish alliance in 1580s, and other populations that mixed with Native Americans in the Caribbean, Suriname, French Guinea, and many other locations. As detailed by Richard and Sally Price, the Saramankan maroon communities of Suriname maintain today a complex African-and-indigenous hybrid social and linguistic culture. The fantasy of marronage—of taking flight from slavery into liberty—represents an essential dream of the New World.

To maroon one's way from slavery to freedom represents an effort to cast one's body into the sea of history and swim by one's own power. As philosopher Neil Roberts writes in *Freedom as Marronage* (2015), this action "is a multidimensional, constant act of flight." In Roberts' view, flight-into-marronage captures "modernity's underside." Building on Glissant's writings, Roberts develops a "marronage philosophy [that] runs counter to the idea of fixed, determinate endings." For Roberts, the unfixedness of marronage rejects Kantian philosophical ideas of freedom and autonomy. In a saltier, oceanic key, unfixedness gestures toward maritime connection and mobility. Acts of flight, escape, and radical difference buoy up Roberts' critique of Enlightenment political philosophy. These ideas also speak to the destabilizing process of exchanging solid ground for liquid sea. Glissant describes the birth of global modernity through the contrast between the classical Mediterranean, "an inner sea surrounded by lands," and the modern Caribbean, "a sea that explodes the scattered lands into an arc." In the New World's "sea that diffracts," human culture assumes maritime multiplicity.

Wet globalization links the flight into radical freedom described by Glissant and Roberts with the re-suturing of the global ecology into a "New Pangea" described by Lewis and Maslin. This premodern Anthropocene—the world humans built, intentionally and not, from the late fifteenth century forward—relies on and is unimaginable without the structural movement and violence of the sea.

5 SEA POETRY I: ADAMASTOR AS WARNING AND GATE

Sea poetry enters the World Ocean through a gate. During early modern wet globalization, that gate shifted from the Pillars of Hercules to Adamastor's Cape of Storms.

The Pillars of Hercules straddle the saltwater gap between Africa and Iberia, opening between the vast Atlantic Ocean and the landlocked Mediterranean Sea. The northern pillar, Calpe Mons, has long been identified as the Rock of Gibraltar. Some debate remains about the location of the southern pillar, Abila Mons, though it is probably Monte Hacho in Ceuta, Morocco, which makes the span of roughly 13 miles (23 km) a narrow watery border between Europe and North Africa. Classical myth describes the Pillars as marking the straits inside which Hercules limited his labors, or in alternate traditions, as a gateway that Hercules either blasted through the Atlas mountains (according to Seneca) or created when he dragged Iberia and Africa closer together in order to protect the Med from the monsters of the Atlantic (per Diodorus of Sicily). In all these traditions, the Pillars mark an opening and an impossibility. They indicate a boundary between worlds: classical antiquity and the Mediterranean inside, global modernity and the Atlantic outside. The symbolism of the Pillars looms large in Western cultural history. Plato located the drowned kingdom of Atlantis in the open ocean, west of the Pillars. In Dante's *Inferno,* restless Ulysses and his men sail through the Pillars never to return. An engraving of the twin pillars frames the cover of Francis Bacon's *The Great Instauration* (1620), a text that self-consciously announces the New Science in early modern England. These two promontories, which pinch from north and south to compress two seas into narrow straits, epitomized the gate through which classical culture encountered the global ocean. The Pillars of Hercules represent the access to Ocean against which classical Mediterranean culture has traditionally been defined.

Despite the symbolic force of the Pillars, whose mythic inscription reads, *Ne plus ultra* ("nothing beyond this point"), Mediterranean sailors have ventured beyond them into the Atlantic for as long as we have historical evidence. Archeologist Barry Cunliffe has documented extensive maritime trade connections between the Atlantic coast and the Mediterranean, starting long before the classical period. The modern Spanish city of Cádiz, located just west of the Pillars on the Iberian coast, sits atop the Phoenician settlement of Gadir, over three millennia old. All four of

Columbus' voyages to the New World left from outside the Pillars of Hercules: two voyages left from Cádiz, and two from smaller ports slightly farther west. The Portuguese expeditions that broadly parallel Columbus', including Vasco da Gama's voyage that would produce the first European landfall on India, left from the port of Belem, just downriver from Lisbon, facing the Atlantic at the mouth of the Tagus River. The ancient conception of the Pillars of Hercules as a barrier needs revision on both the symbolic and the navigational levels. Prevailing west winds inside the straits would have hindered Atlantic-bound ships, but ancient navigators regularly used this passage as an opening onto the radically different tidal, wind, and current patterns of the deep ocean. The Pillars shift between barrier and gate, as Holy Roman Emperor Charles V recognized in 1520 when he inverted the classical "Ne plus ultra" and took as his own personal motto "Plus ultra"—more beyond. Charles' open-gated image of the Pillars appears today on the Spanish flag, among other places.

The transformation of the Pillars from barrier to gate did not happen arbitrarily. Navigational techniques and the physical geography of the sea made global oceanic expansion possible. New sea routes guided European ships around the world during and after the fifteenth century. Perhaps the most famous sea routes of the early modern period followed the *volta do mar,* or *volta do mar largo*, a technique by which mariners sailed west out into the Atlantic from the Canaries or Cape Verde Islands in order to locate trade winds that would take them northeast toward Europe, west into the Caribbean, or, in the later sixteenth century, south around the African Cape. Portuguese sailors also used this "turn to the sea" technique in the Pacific to pioneer the Manila Galleon trade route between Mexico, the Philippines, and China. Rounding the southern tip of Africa, like rounding Cape Horn on the southern tip of the Americas, represented on a global scale what the Pillars of Hercules epitomized in the Mediterranean. These geographic features mark difficult maritime passages that must be mastered by particular techniques, after which the route becomes a functioning gateway. In the Portuguese East India trade, Bartholomew Diaz pioneered the rounding of the African Cape into the Indian Ocean in 1488. A decade later, Vasco da Gama established one of the most important sea routes in the early modern world by completing the full voyage from Lisbon to India. The *carreira da India* that he pioneered has been described as the "lifeline" of the early modern Portuguese maritime empire. Columbus' route to the Caribbean connected Europe to the New World, and Vasco da Gama's eastbound passage provided an efficient maritime connection to the wealthy kingdoms of Asia. The two explorers traveled in opposite directions, but both of these epoch-defining voyages relied on the physical geography of winds, currents, and capes.

Navigating these passages wrecked many early modern ships. As Josiah Blackmore has observed, the Portuguese literature of shipwreck responds ambivalently to the massive expansion of the maritime empire and its harrowing cost in ships and sailors. The essential literary text of early modern Europe's oceanic turn, Luís Vaz de Camões' *The Lusiads* (1572), builds a poetic epic from the story of Vasco da Gama's voyage. Modeled on classical epics such as Homer's *Odyssey* and Virgil's *Aeneid*, *The Lusiads* substitutes maritime travel for heroic combat. In what would become the national epic of Portugal, shipwreck and empire comingle. "In the Camonian understanding of epic," Blackmore observes, "disaster exists coterminously with an espousal of imperialist ideologies, so there is no cause and effect between the two: empire exists alongside shipwreck, alongside its own undoing." The poem's most striking symbol of this entanglement of disaster and maritime expansion is the Titan Adamastor, a literalization of Africa's southern Cape, which we now call the Cape of Good Hope. As Blackmore notes, "Adamastor is . . . shipwreck awesomely incarnate." The more-than-human figure represents both the natural obstacle of the Cape and also the price in suffering exacted from sailors enduring the world-changing sea route. By replacing the narrow gates of the Pillars of Hercules with the hostile rage of Adamastor in the South Atlantic, Camões presents via his lovesick Titan the lure, cost, and nonhuman violence of wet globalization.

Literalizing the first Portuguese name for the southern tip of Africa, the *Cabo de Tormentas* (Cape of Storms), Adamastor appears in the poem as an "immense shape" that blocks out the sky. While the clouds assume Titanic form, Camões emphasizes the opacity of the mariner's encounter with the southeastern boundary of Atlantic waters:

So fearful it looked, so overpowering,
It put great terror in our hearts;
The dark, invisible waters roared
As if frustrated, pounding on some reef.

The oceanic world names itself through terror, darkness, and the pounding sound of unseen waters. The poem presents Adamastor slowly emerging from invisibility to partial comprehension. Interpreting the surf's struggle against the reef as frustration (Portuguese *em vão*, in vain) anticipates the way Adamastor will transform the physical features of the ocean into erotic forces. The Titan himself emerges from darkness and inchoate longing:

Grotesque and of enormous stature
With heavy jowls, and an unkempt beard
Scowling from shrunken, hollow eyes,
In complexion earthy and pale,
Its hair grizzled and matted with clay,
Its mouth coal black, teeth yellow with decay.

The Cape-Titan presents "earthy" (*terrana*) features in a maritime surround. Like Shakespeare's earth-ocean monster Caliban in *The Tempest*, Adamastor combines features of the earth (clay, coal) with evidence of the sea's touch (grizzled hair, decayed teeth). The Titan erupts into view, "booming from the ocean's depths," but he also takes the form of a rocky promontory overlooking the turbulent waters of the

Cape. The split vision above and beneath the ocean's surface replicates a swimmer's view of the sea, one eye above and the other below. Adamastor's turbulent mixing of land and sea marks him as an allegory of elemental struggle and violence. The pounding of surf on stone defines him. The creature's "dreadful form" terrifies the mariners as his appearance marks their exit from the familiar waters of the Atlantic.

On a larger scale than the Pillars of Hercules, Adamastor's Cape represents a boundary and articulates a warning. The monster's voice attempts to force the Portuguese fleet back. "Because you have desecrated nature's / Secrets and the mysteries of the deep," the Titan cautions, "Hear from me now what retribution / Fate proscribes for your insolence." The wages of Adamastor are shipwreck, and in Blackmore's reading of this scene the destruction of Portuguese ships at the Cape of Storms articulates the cost of maritime empire. David Quint, in a persuasive analysis of this episode, notes that the Titan appears at the same time as the mariners encounter hostile natives, so that Adamastor might also represent the indigenous people of Africa. "My cape will be implacably hostile," the Titan insists to the mariners. In sailing to this point and beyond, Vasco da Gama's fleet parallels the reckless urge to explore that brought Dante's Ulysses outside the Pillars of Hercules. The alien nature of the seas of the southern hemisphere appears in both Dante and Camões through the sight of "new heavens" that include the Southern Cross in place of the familiar constellations of the North. As the mariners press around the Cape, they place themselves under the sign of Adamastor. "Year by year your fleets will meet / Shipwreck," the monster proclaims. His curse echoes that of Polyphemus in the *Odyssey*; both da Gama and Odysseus gain mobility by escaping nonhuman hands, but the mobility they gain includes the disorienting push of the sea.

Camões' Titan distinguishes himself from Homer's Cyclops because he suffers from environmental proximity. As his allegory of unrequited desire demonstrates, Adamastor allegorizes not simply shipwreck but also the doomed love of the sea that motivates mariners throughout history. Adamastor's longing for Tethys, goddess of the sea, anticipates the ocean-love that would define Romantic and post-Romantic sea poetry. John Masefield's famous lyric poem "Sea Fever" (1902) captures something of the Titan's longing and fear of the enticing alien waters. "I must go down to the seas again," rhapsodizes Masefield, "for the call of the running tide, / Is a wild call and a clear call that may not be denied." Adamastor's desire for the sea-goddess Tethys matches Masefield's longing for the sea. What Masefield loves, however, Camões fears. For both Titan and poet, the ocean inflames a dangerous and unattainable love. Adamastor, after attempting to enlist the assistance of Tethys' mother, describes the ocean's full erotic glory:

> Tethys approached, with her glorious
> Face and her naked, matchless body;
> Like a madman I ran, with arms

Outstretched, to her who was my
Soul's life, heart's joy, body's prayer,
Kissing her lovely eyes, her cheeks, her hair.

The Titan's fantasy of immersion joins the abstractions of desire—soul, heart, prayer—to the physical features of the sea nymph's eyes, cheeks, and hair. But since saltwater makes up the substance of Tethys' body, the giant splashes through sea-foam and ends up embracing only his own rocky form: "I found myself hugging a hillside." The final freeze-frame of Adamastor's futile longing captures the immobility of rocks in churning surf. "The gods molded my great bulk," he laments, "Into this remote promontory; / And of all tortures, the most agonizing / Is that Tethys surrounds me, tantalizing" (*Me anda . . . cercando*, Tethys walks around me). Anticipating by inversion the orgiastic finale of *The Lusiads*, in which Vasco da Gama and his mariners sport with sea nymphs on the Island of Love in the Indian Ocean, Adamastor represents a sea fever that never stops burning. The epic of sea travel rotates itself around the still point of the Titan's longing and its "tantalizing" proximity to the surf.

Adamastor represents the painful love sailors feel for the sea and the destructive consequences of that desire. Camões' portrait of the Titan suggests that his attitude toward maritime travel spans celebration and trepidation. The Portuguese sailors assume heroic status by turning toward hostile and alien sea routes, but the always-moving waters never return their love. At the end of the Canto preceding

Adamastor's, the epic lingers with the anti-maritime warnings of the Old Man of Belem, who sends the Portuguese fleet into the Atlantic with a curse that in many ways anticipates that of the African Titan. "The devil take the man," the Old Man intones, "who first put / Dry wood on the waves with a sail!" This terrestrial voice speaks from a rival classical tradition to that of Odysseus the sailor. Classical writers such as Plato and Hesiod distrusted the sea. For Plato, the ideal city should be located at least eleven miles inland, "for the sea, although an agreeable, is a dangerous companion, and a highway of strange morals and manners as well as commerce." Hesiod in *Works and Days* warns Mediterranean sailors only to venture during seasons of reliable weather in spring and summer, and he further cautions that sea travel is always risky. "Do not put all your means of livelihood," he advises, "inside hollow ships." The Old Man of Belem speaks for this tradition when he treats the sea as an environment of "Wretched circumstance." To stay dry in Camões' epic world might mean to stay safe and stable—but it also means to refuse the hero's gambit and its promised reward. In framing the voyage between two alternative curses—Adamastor's, which indicates that the price of travel is shipwreck, and the Old Man's, which emphasizes the folly of embarkation—*The Lusiads* treats sea travel as the defining and confining feature of the early modern Portuguese state. Like Adamastor, the mariners are surrounded by waters that tantalize and threaten. Unlike the rock-bound Titan, they employ those waters as a means to a mobile end.

6 SAILORS: A TECHNOLOGICAL HISTORY

Sailors Are Cyborgs

I don't mean that the old salts you can still sometimes find in harborside bars match all the features of Donna Haraway's famous "A Cyborg Manifesto" (1984), that "ironic political myth faithful to feminism, socialism, and materialism." In fact, of Haraway's terms only materialism seems a good match for most mariners, since sailors are, above all, practical laborers who know what knots to tie and how to lash material things to each other. Maritime socialism might appear in the entwined community-feeling that Joseph Conrad imagines as the bonds between each "one of us." Marcus Rediker even argues that the golden age of Atlantic piracy represents an era of radical social democratic experiment, with pirate ships being both more violent and more democratic than either European monarchies or navy ships, which were manned mostly by unwilling crews. But Haraway's feminism skews away from the man-machine hybrid identities of sailors, given that, historically, being a seaman meant joining a mostly male society—such as that in Melville's *Moby-Dick*, which idealized the male marriage between Ishmael and Queequeg and rhapsodized the image of a circle of whalemen squeezing sperm oil together. There's often something queer and loving about maritime masculinity.

The cyborg identity of mariners may depart from some elements of Haraway's late-twentieth-century political theory, but it matches her calls for "couplings between organism and machine" and the formation of a "technological polis." Sailors love boats and rigging, and the culture of maritime labor embraces a powerful romance between humans and technology. The love of sea-craft echoes from Odysseus building his own ship on Calypso's island to a prefatory poem written to Captain John Smith's 1627 *Sea Grammar,* which gave the English language the word "technology" for the first time. (Smith, whose military rank came from service in the army, cribbed most of his sailor talk from ex-pirate Henry Mainwaring, whose *Sea-mans Dictionary* was written before Smith's book but published over a decade later.) As readers of historical maritime fiction and practical mariners know, sailors share a private language that entwines human bodies with nonhuman tools. Haraway names her cyborg a "myth of political identity" in service of which "stories" and "writing" are essential tools. Sailors also comprise political myth-makers, and their tools are sailcloth, rope, and hulls—along with stories, shanties, cant terms, and many forms of writing.

The origins of sailing float in the depths of prehistory. The oldest image of a ship appears in the Middle East sometime around 5000 BCE. Maritime exchanges between Persian Gulf cultures and the Indus Valley date from around 3000 BCE, and images of boats with square sails heading before the wind upriver on the Nile date to around 3500 BCE. It seems certain that human cultures used boats for local travel, probably powered by oars, from an earlier date, and the fairly simple innovation of hoisting a sail to assist in downwind locomotion cannot have be far behind. Anyone who has spent time in a canoe or other small craft on a breezy day knows that any surface that shows a broad face to the wind, including a human back, can enable moving air to move a boat. The long history of the adaptation of wind power to maritime travel represents millennia of reiteration and refinement of this basic practice, from ancient river barges to the latest World Cup yachts. The tools of the sailor, including spreading a wide area of sail before the wind and adding steering devices such as keels or a rudder, focus the impersonal circulation of winds around the globe and transform them into directed motive force.

Sailing Large

The oldest and simplest form of sailing simply positions a boat before the wind, so that pressure on the sail drives the craft downwind. For this purpose, square sails were the simplest to make and handle, and they could provide a large surface area for maximum force. Flat-bottomed boats with no keel were practical for river channels, such as the Nile, which feature shallow water and little need to steer, while sharper keels and rudders were required for more involved navigation. The great limitation of sailing "large" before the wind is that you can only move in the direction the wind is blowing. Many ancient boats carried oars for movement against or across the wind, and sailing would mostly require favorable weather. Developments in steering, rudders, and keels, as well as maneuverable sails, allowed vessels to steer at oblique angles to the wind. Sailing into the wind required the development of different sail technologies. Global sailing, including the transoceanic voyages of Columbus and Vasco da Gama, entailed following the prevailing winds and currents that make up the ocean gyres, so these world-encircling voyages could rely mostly on square sails presenting their surface area large athwart the wind. In many ways, these ships, though they represented state-of-the-art world-changing technology in the late fifteenth century, operated through the same principle as the earliest Egyptian barges that floated grain upriver with the wind in the fourth millennium BCE. The interface between ship, water, and wind combines simple physics with a process of adaptation that continues today.

Sailing by and Large: The Lateen Sail

Among the many innovations in the long history of sailing, few are as storied and controversial as the development of the triangular or lateen sail. The name "lateen" derives from the word Latin, but historically these sails, which enabled ships to sail closer to the wind (i.e., farther upwind, rather than only in the direction that the wind blows), were associated with Arab mariners in the Middle Ages. A thorough study by I. C. Campbell (1995) suggests that the technology seems likely to have emerged from the development of leech lines that could reshape square sails in order to make them catch the wind more efficiently at an angle. Campbell reviews the evidence for the presence of lateen sails in the ancient Mediterranean, where these sails became standard for the Byzantine navy by the sixth century CE. Comparable sail shapes appeared among Malay sailors and also in the Indian Ocean, where they were probably useful in sailing obliquely against the prevailing monsoon winds on the return voyage from East Africa to India. It's not clear, however, if the Portuguese sailors who arrived into the millennia-old Indian Ocean trading network in the late fifteenth century introduced lateen sails they had brought from the Mediterranean, or if they encountered variations on the sail among Asian craft. As Campbell emphasizes, triangular sails were an obvious practical choice for greater maneuverability upwind or for navigation close inshore. These sails may well have developed independently in multiple maritime centers, including the Mediterranean, Indian Ocean, and the Pacific basins. Only some maritime innovations, such as the outrigger canoe developed by Polynesian navigators, were distinctive and appeared only in one location—though in the case of the outrigger canoe, that area was the largest ocean basin on the globe, and the outrigger facilitated the largest-scale maritime migration in prehistory, through which Asian peoples populated southeast Asia, Australia, and the islands of the Pacific.

The presence of lateen sails on European ships during the Age of Exploration has led to exaggerating the importance of these sails as innovations that facilitated transoceanic travel. The standard rigging for da Gama's Portuguese carracks and for Columbus' ships included two forward masts flying square sails and a lateen on the mizzen. This arrangement helped navigate the Indian Ocean monsoons as well as supporting inshore sailing, but in general long haul voyages sailed downwind behind square rigs. Oceangoing ships would of course have carried both kinds of sails, and a ship might fly different canvas during long downwind passages as opposed to what they would use to make port or sail in a variable breeze.

Gyre Navigation

The largest components in the cyborg assemblage that comprises the collective body of the earliest global sailors are the ocean gyres. Each of the major ocean basins contains a continuously circulating system of prevailing winds and currents. The circulation of the gyres rotates clockwise in the northern hemisphere and counterclockwise in the southern;

the eastbound Antarctic Circumpolar Current roars unimpeded by land below forty degrees south longitude around the globe, forming a structural floor beneath the system of gyres, at least when world maps locate the south pole at the bottom. For Anglophone readers, the North Atlantic Gyre makes the most familiar example: the Canary Current forms its eastern boundary, flowing south from Europe toward Africa's coastal islands. From there the waters and winds flow west with the North Atlantic Equatorial Current into the Caribbean Sea. These currents guided Columbus' ships from southern Spain to the New World, as they subsequently guided most early modern transatlantic shipping, from the Spanish *flota* to the West African slave trade. From the Caribbean, the gyre turns north and then east in the Gulf Stream, in which five hundred times as much water as the flow of the Amazon River surges out of the Caribbean through the narrow Straits of Florida and up the southeastern coast of what is now the United States. The current then bends to the east as the North Atlantic Current, which returns to Europe and completes the circle.

Would You Rather Be a Sailor or a Swimmer?

Sometime not long after World War II, the human relation with the ocean changed. The dominant metaphoric relationship between humans and the sea had long been seafaring, as shown in stories from Homer's *Odyssey* through to Hemingway's *Old Man and the Sea* (1952). Swimming had been mostly a survival tactic and tool for soldiers, salvage divers, and a few other specialists. Following the Romantic reimagination of the ocean, however, immersion became at first sublime and transformative and eventually a popular recreation. Beach culture in the West began with medicinal dunking of often female patients in cold saltwater that was thought to rebalance bodily functions. But after the mid-twentieth century the beach became synonymous with leisure, pleasure, and a respite from urban life. The vacation homes in New Jersey that were swamped by Superstorm Sandy in 2012 sat atop barrier islands first developed as building lots in the postwar boom years. Many vacationers on the Atlantic shore were sailors as well as swimmers, but immersion would become the normative engagement with the coastal ocean over the next several generations.

When sailing became secondary rather than primary, the human physical relationship with the ocean become embodied as well as technological. Sailors thrive through technological tinkering; swimmers survive through practiced motions of their limbs and torso. The shift from mechanical alliance to physical immersion suggests a variation on the famous closing motto of Haraway's manifesto. She rejects the metaphysical by intoning, "I would rather be a cyborg than a goddess." Sailor-centric nostalgia of the sort that made Patrick O'Brian's twenty-novel saga about the Royal Navy during the Napoleonic Wars an international sensation might insist that

"I would rather be a sailor than a swimmer." Many sailors, more pointedly, might support Joseph Conrad's position that the displacement of the sailing ship by first steam and later diesel represents the loss of a peculiarly beautiful practice. "And the sailing of any fine vessel afloat is an art," Conrad writes in *The Mirror of the Sea*, "whose fine form seems already receding from us on its way to the overshadowed Valley of Oblivion." Conrad's nostalgia and O'Brian's literary ventriloquism mark the last gasps of sailor-culture, a cyborg world in which the complex vocabulary of sails and ropes had not yet calcified into metaphor. To sail inside what is now mostly allegory—to labor in a context in which "by and large" refers to ways of orientation in relation to a headwind or following wind—means reinhabiting the centrality of the sailor in the long saga of the human relationship with the World Ocean.

Discounting some dabbling aboard small craft and windsurfing as a kid, I'm a swimmer, and this book builds toward a pro-immersion celebration of swimming as bodily encounter with the twenty-first-century global environment. But, especially on brisk afternoon in early fall, when I hurry my chilled body into the fluid body of Long Island Sound to feel how the water holds late summer's warmth, I look in admiration at sails framed taut by the breeze. Most of the sailboats in my bay in Connecticut are the steep triangles of Bermuda-rigged 420s used by college sailing teams, plus a few different larger or smaller craft piloted by my neighbors. There's not much maritime labor in my town's coastal waters, except for one local guy who drags for clams, running a diesel engine. It's swimmer's water today, as well as a playground for kayakers and occasionally a Jet Ski or two. But when I see the sails darting out past Half-Tide Rock toward open water with the green ribbon of Long Island just visible in the horizon, I feel a slight tug of what Conrad feels about the fine lost art of cyborg sailing. Sometimes we miss the things we have lost, even if we love the water we swim in now.

7 INTERLUDE: PORT OF NEW YORK

On April 26, 1956, the cargo ship *Ideal-X* left Newark, New Jersey, with fifty-eight identically shaped rectangular metal boxes on deck. The vessel docked five days later in Houston, where fifty-eight trucks took the containers to their destinations. That voyage changed the modern world. It also doomed the Port of New York.

In 1929, Federico García Lorca arrived in Manhattan as a young student and emerging writer. His volume *Poet in New York*, published posthumously in 1940, recorded the turbulent experience of the Andalusian writer encountering the modern global city.

Together the Port and the Poet reveal the pathways through which the preeminent city of the United States turned away from its historic connection to the sea during the twentieth century. The Port hides New York's oceanic past, while the Poet reflects its wet traces.

It's a sad story, but there's a glimmer of light at the end.

The City's Wet Feet

Today the southern coastline of Manhattan island, as it existed before European contact, lies several blocks from the water's edge. Seventeenth-century maps do not show the land beneath Stuyvesant Town, Battery Park City, the Freedom Tower, or much of the lower east side around South Street Seaport. These areas, which extend the city's coastline out from the southern tip of the island into both the East and Hudson Rivers, comprise "made land," or industrial fill dumped into the rivers, on top of which wharves, docks, and eventually city blocks were constructed. As historian Kurt Schlichting shows in *Waterfront Manhattan* (2018), the expansion of city into the rivers took place via public-private partnerships: the city sold submerged land to private developers, who filled the riverfront in and built atop the newly made land. The most recent public-private partnership near lower Manhattan's coast, the elevated park and greenway of the High Line, which, since its opening in 2009, has become one of the city's most popular tourist sites, continues a tradition of creating public infrastructure by partnering with private investment that has shaped the island's maritime borders since the eighteenth century.

The longshoremen and dockworkers who unloaded cargo in the Port of New York in the nineteenth and early twentieth centuries worked atop what was once water. The unruly culture of maritime labor underscores much of what has long been implied by the term "downtown." Dockworkers, sailors, and the ships and cargoes that came to lower Manhattan during this period contributed to the unhygienic overcrowding in the lower East Side that outraged visitors such as Charles Dickens in 1842. As shipping moved from docks along the East River and South Street across town to Greenwich Village and the Hudson waterfront in the late nineteenth century, immigrant laborers and labor-intensive dock work followed. Reformers such as Jacob Riis saw downtown tenements as problems to be identified, torn down, and rebuilt by following new designs.

"Christmas on the Hudson"

For the poet, New York's waterfront presents a fantasia of violence and motion. The country boy from dry Andalusia sees the city's proximity to the salt-infused river and the maze of its maritime downtown as threats of entanglement and potential ambush. He looks at the river and tries to make sense of what he sees:

> That gray sponge!
> That sailor whose throat was just cut.
> That great river.
> Those dark boundaries of the breeze.
> That keen blade, my love, that keen blade.

For García Lorca, the Hudson in winter absorbs everything into its blank immensity. The dead sailor and the blade that cut his flesh echo the river and the breeze. Natural forces and human violence balance each other across the keen edge. In New York's maritime boundary, he finds the "world alone in the lonely sky" and "This alone: river's mouth." For the poet, only the great river matches the city.

Longshoreman's End

The Port Authority of New York and New Jersey was established in 1921 to manage commercial access to the region and coordinate issues of concern to both states. In 1947 the Port Authority obtained control of land on the waterfront of Newark, New Jersey, across the bay from lower Manhattan. In 1952, construction began on new piers and cargo sheds on six acres in Newark, an open expanse that would have been impossible to find in crowded Manhattan or maritime Brooklyn. In 1955, Newark and Elizabeth launched what would be the largest public maritime infrastructure investment in the history of New York Harbor. The engineers and urban planners did not know it, but they were building for container transport, which would use the space for mechanized docks and open back lots where trucks could load containers onto flatbeds. Port Newark and its sister Port Elizabeth would soon become the busiest container port on the east coast of the United States. The Port of New York in lower Manhattan, which for centuries had been the most economically important point of maritime exchange in the nation, collapsed in a generation. The docks, wharves, and made land of the southern point of the island gave way to the open spaces and reclaimed marshlands of Newark, with its close access to the New Jersey Turnpike and the interstate highway system.

"Sleepless City (Brooklyn Bridge Nocturne)"

Sometimes the poet heads downtown, so that he stares up at the Brooklyn Bridge where it arcs above the East River. From there he sees things that make him afraid. He dreams of new possibilities and glimpses the global future toward which the narrow point of Manhattan island aims its prow:

> Watch out! Watch out! Watch out!
> Those still marked by claws and cloudburst,
> that boy who cries because he doesn't know about the
> invention of bridges
> or that corpse that has nothing more than its head and
> one shoe—

From his view of New York beneath the gleaming bridge, the poet peers into a world of loss. The "invention of bridges" promises a future unmarked by the "claws" of creatures that emerge from the water or the "cloudburst" that wets the streets. In this unsettled city, "no one sleeps"—or, in Spanish,

"No duerme nadie," which might also mean that no one dreams. It's a broken world, populated by bodies with no heads and shoes without feet. It's a world confined by water, by sleeplessness, and by exposure.

What We Talk about When We Talk about Newark

The container revolution, like many aspects of late-twentieth-century globalization, displaced human labor as it made commerce more efficient. During the transition period of the 1960s, the International Longshoreman's Association (ILA) bargained hard and often successfully for its increasingly workless membership. The shipping industry quietly paid the wages of aging ILA members whether they worked or not, and as ILA members retired the workforce dwindled. After three centuries during which off-loading cargo was a major source of employment on the New York waterfront, the container revolution hollowed out the ranks of longshoremen and replaced them with steel boxes.

The photographer and cultural theorist Allan Sekula, whose multimedia work represents one of the most powerful engagements with the container revolution, suggests that containers superimposed impersonal modernity on top of the human heterogeneity of the port. The advent of almost-fully automated container ports in places like Rotterdam and

Shanghai, both of which feature in the 2010 film *The Forgotten Space* that Sekula co-made with Noël Burch, virtually erases the human worker from a crucial nexus of global capitalism. In his brilliant 1995 study *Fish Story*, Sekula notes that the modern port has destroyed the historical relationship between human workers and the sea: "modernity dissolves the edifying unity of the classical maritime panorama." Ancient and resonant scenes of maritime labor, from fishermen clustering in portside bars, to Odysseus steering between Scylla and Charybdis, to Captain Ahab chasing the white whale into the Sea of Japan, gave way in the 1960s to a mechanized system of interlocking machine parts. No rowdy longshoremen wander the docks of Port Newark today. South Street Seaport teems with hipster bars and expensive condos.

The water-land interface in twenty-first-century Newark does not only hold steel containers and mechanized lifts. The area also abuts historic wetlands, which have been massively polluted by industry but still boast a complex human and inhuman ecology. As Robert Sullivan notes in *The Meadowlands* (1998), the area's swampland consists of a semi-wilderness next to the city, which has become "through negligence, through exploitation, and through its own chaotic persistence, explorable again." Sullivan's partly ironic description of the postindustrial landscape as "Big Sky Country East" masks his sincere, almost Thoreauvian evocation of a damaged landscape that still offers much to intrepid explorers. The old picaresque Port of New York has vanished, but in its place we find Sullivan's garbage dump sublime and Sekula's containerized vision of techno-modernity. We need to learn to love, see, and touch these alien futures.

"Ode to Walt Whitman"

Few poets come to New York without seeking the ghost of Walt Whitman. García Lorca found Walt down among the docks, among the workers, in a soon-to-vanish world of masculinity, labor, and partly concealed eroticism:

> Not for a moment, Adam of blood, Macho,
> man alone at sea, Walt Whitman, lovely old man,
> because on penthouse roofs,
> gathered at bars,
> emerging in bunches from the sewers,
> trembling between the legs of chauffeurs,
> or spinning on dance floors wet with absinthe,
> the faggots, Walt Whitman, point you out.

Modernist poets from Elizabeth Bishop to Pablo Neruda have looked to Whitman's radical embrace of novelty and the poetics of the everyday. Many queer poets find in his visions of physicality an erotics of masculine power. García Lorca finds both sexuality and modernity in his "Adam of blood" who appears present among the men "gathered at bars" and "emerging in bunches from the sewers." But in imagining his

Whitman-muse as a "man alone at sea," the poet also locates the poetics of the city in the maritime milieu that would soon vanish from downtown.

The View from the High Line

When I walk on the High Line from my favorite Chelsea locavore restaurant on West 20th Street down toward the glorious outdoor sculpture gardens of the Whitney Museum of American Art, the Hudson gleams over my shoulder. Longshoremen and tall ships have long since departed. The latest private-public partnership has transformed the old elevated rail line, which between 1934 and the 1960s carried tons upon tons of maritime goods up the West Side, into a greenway that has been a massive boon to downtown real estate values. The High Line, with its public art and trendy food carts, does not resemble the maritime world it displaced. But it's nice still to catch a gleam off the moving Hudson while walking today along its postmodern cityscape.

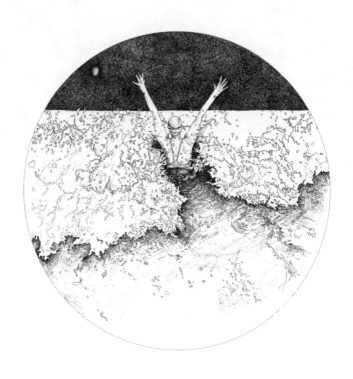

8 SEA POETRY II: THE SEA IN EMILY DICKINSON

From the ship on which Richard Henry Dana sailed round Cape Horn in 1836 to the Black Ball ocean "liners" that provided a regular passenger service between New York and Liverpool starting in 1818, the nineteenth century saw a massive expansion of global maritime transportation. With more ships came more oceanic thinking. W. H. Auden's proclamation that nineteenth-century Romanticism "invented" the modern idea of the Sea appears somewhat exaggerated, but Romantic sea poetry helped transform the navigational set pieces of premodern literature into a poetic obsession with the human-ocean relationship. With Romanticism, the sea changed from horror into truth. The Alien touched the Core. Even the master-mariner Odysseus views immersion as suffering, but Lord Byron and Walt Whitman embrace the waters as ecstasy and revelation. Byron celebrates his intimate love for saltwater from "youthful sports" to the "pleasing fear" of his maturity. Whitman seeks "amorous wet" in the "crooked inviting fingers" of the surf. Sea poems by canonical Romantics from Wordsworth and Coleridge to Keats and Shelley remain well known, and Jonathan Raban's *Oxford Book of the Sea* (1992) also includes ocean-focused prose snippets from Jane Austen, Charles Lamb, Charles Dickens, Edgar Allen Poe, and many others. The nineteenth century, with its expansions in literacy and the circulation of printed books, fomented the poetics of sea fever.

The sea poet I select to represent this salt-drenched era is a spinster from Amherst, Massachusetts. Emily Dickinson's sprawling corpus of experimental verse is not often central to compilations of nineteenth-century sea poetry. Raban includes only one poem of hers in his anthology. But Dickinson's use of the sea as symbol and force, imaginative pressure and inhuman immensity, makes her an ideal poet of Ocean. Byron and Whitman claim greater intimacy with the waters, and Melville and Dana certainly deploy more salty terms, but Dickinson's visionary sea poetics captures Ocean as the physical and cultural force that reshaped the nineteenth-century globe.

The sea appears more often in Dickinson's poetry than many who think of her as a bucolic or melancholic garden poet might think. The ocean surfaces distinctly in her language, sometimes as metaphor or oblique reference. Viewed from an offshore blue humanities perspective, her sea poems roll toward land like California breakers after their thousand-mile fetch across the Pacific. Her ocean unfurls itself in distinct surges, each building upon and crashing into the others.

Sea as the Opposite of Land

Looking directly at a thing makes it strange. Few Anglophone poets equal Dickinson's ability to refract strangeness into language. She sees the ocean as Alien in its vastness and ungraspable fluidity:

> An Everywhere of Silver
> With Ropes of Sand
> To keep it from effacing
> The Track called Land—

The lyric's visionary gleam emerges from its sensory obliqueness, a turning-away that defines both the "silver" glisten of the water's surface and the "Everywhere" across which the ocean's bulk spreads. The one-stanza poem opens with silver and slowly backs its way toward more tangible things, in the "Ropes of Sand," and their rhyming echo "Track called Land." Within the microclimate of the poem's scant four lines, Dickinson conjures oceanic difference as alien pressure. The sea's contact with shore threatens to erase human habitations. Our terrestrial home becomes temporary, a "Track" that only can be "called" solid. Ocean in this poem opposes the Land it effaces; a silver flash of saltwater reminds us of the world in which we do not live.

The Sea as Alien spirit appears fairly often in Dickinson's poems. In the well-known lyric "'Hope' is the thing with feathers," the title of which contributes to the popular misimagination of Dickinson as an author of poetic Hallmark Cards, Ocean lurks in the final stanza's glimpse of "the strangest Sea" that "never—in Extremity, / [. . .] asked a crumb—of me." The alterity of the Sea echoes the strangeness of the poem; quotable lines about happy birds and flowers unravel into complexity. In "A bird came down the walk," the bucolic milieu of bird, worm, beetle, and garden dissolves into an Oceanic final stanza that gestures toward immensity beyond comprehension:

> [. . .] Oars divide the Ocean,
> Too silver for a seam,
> Or Butterflies, off Banks of Noon,
> Leap, plashless as they swim.

The indivisible ocean, named by its silver color, reimagines butterflies in their garden as silent swimmers whose plashing lacks only water. Likewise, the anti-marital poem, "She rose to His Requirement" also builds up to an oceanic final stanza: "It lay unmentioned—as the Sea / Develope Pearl and Weed, / But only to Himself—be known / The Fathom they abide—." In these lyrics, an initial human scenario, pastoral or domestic, juxtaposes itself against the Sea as unanswerable Alien, fathomless in its depths.

Dickinson's poetic imagination casts the Silver otherness "Everywhere" as space of fear and desire. To her landlocked self, Ocean challenges and spurs imaginative creation:

I never saw a Moor.
I never saw the Sea—
Yet I know how the Heather looks
And what a Billow be—

These two natural vistas, inhospitable Moor and swelling Sea, together define the farthest reaches of poetry's geography. To know the ocean as moving waves passing among and through each other—to know waters being "Billow"—requires the poet to place herself outside familiar confines and hospitable spaces. In making her poetry a vehicle for more-than-human complexity, Dickinson makes oceanic vastness one of her most potent and flexible metaphors.

Sea as Lure

The spinster poet's most ecstatically erotic verses envision the "Wild nights" of sexual "luxury" in terms of over-going maritime technologies of orientation:

Futile—the winds—
To a Heart in port—
Done with the Compass—
Done with the Chart!

Enclosed in an erotic and emotional harbor, she needs neither direction-finding Compass nor route-plotting Chart to locate herself on the sea's expanse. Overflowing with ecstasy and immersion, she inverts and masculinizes her erotic metaphor. No longer her lover's "port," she instead becomes an aggressive principle of penetrative anchoring:

> Rowing in Eden—
> Ah—the Sea!
> Might I but moor—tonight
> In thee!

To "moor" in love, in the sea, and in the lover's body, imagines a way that maritime labor—"rowing"—carves out space for human bodies in hostile environments. In the erotic reverie of the lyric, "Eden" becomes "Sea," and both spaces open themselves up to the poet's embrace. The ocean remains alien but has now become an attractive lure, whirling the poet-lover into its salty embrace.

The overt eroticism of "Wild nights" is rare in Dickinson's poetry, but more subtle traces appear elsewhere via the metaphor of the ocean. In "My River runs to Thee," the poet presents a possible romance between herself as River and the ambivalently welcoming Sea. "I'll fetch thee books / From spotted nooks—" she importunes. The ocean's replies are noncommittal, and the poem ends in the question: "*Say* Sea—take me?" The vast ocean welcomes the stream but also threatens to overwhelm its coherent identity. As in "Wild nights," oceanic embrace challenges singular selfhood. A similar tension between alternative forms of identity appears in "Two swimmers wrestled on the spar." The oblique narrative of shipwreck and struggle, with its echoes of the "two spent swimmers that do cling together, / and choke their art" in *Macbeth*, divides itself between two semi-immersed bodies. One swimmer "turned smiling to the land," but the poet's attention fastens on "Oh God! the Other One!" The second swimmer, presumably drowning, captures the visionary attention of the concluding stanza. Having followed the ocean's lure away from land, the second swimmer's face appears "With eyes in death—still begging raised— / And hands—beseeching—thrown!" The drowned man's prayerful attitude, begging and beseeching, suggest that in his final immersion he encounters a higher truth, alien, deadly, desired. Unlike the union of "Wild nights," here the swimmers divide, and only one survives.

Dickinson's most elaborate evocation of the deadly and pleasurable lure of immersion appears in "I started Early—Took my Dog." At twenty-four lines, the poem is one of Dickinson's most sustained efforts. Its six four-line stanzas trace an unusually clear narrative of exploration and encounter. The poet's project of "visit[ing] the Sea" takes in "Mermaids" and "Frigates," but in the key moment of encounter, the Ocean not the human assumes command:

> But no Man moved me—till the Tide
> Went past my simple Shoe—

And past my Apron—and my Belt
And past my Boddice—too—

Informed by the ecstatic union of "Wild nights" and the more oblique rhythms of "My River runs" and "Two swimmers," this poem presents Ocean as suitor, moving up and over the poet's body from Apron to Belt to Boddice. The encounter transforms sexually charged flow into carnivorous fantasy, in which the masculine Tide "made as He would eat me up." The nonhuman movement of Ocean's saltwater body threatens to consume the adventurous poet, and presumably her Dog too. The faithful canine disappears after the first line, but the tone created by the Dog grounds the adventure in domestic exploits. As she withdraws from the beach, the Tide follows with the now-familiar color: "I felt His Silver Heel." But the transformative moment, which revises in a nonhuman direction the unity imagined in the erotic poems, combines poet and Tide into a communal "We" that sweeps over "the solid Town." Together wave and poet flow from the world of Ocean to the world of Humans. In this dry space, the wave finds "No One He seemed to know," and so departs: "with a Mighty look / At me—the Sea withdrew." The encounter over, the poet-adventurer returns to Town with wet feet and knowledge. The wave's departing "Mighty look" fixes an Oceanic hook in her breast, as the receding Tide abandons her in a dry world. Its silver lure, we imagine, will tickle her feet again.

The Hierarchy of Nature

In rushing to the sea, the poet-swimmers of "Wild nights" and "I started Early" seek in the great waters a glimpse of plentitude that exceeds the careful demarcations of life on land. In Dickinson's vision of natural power, Ocean represents an alien mastery. The Sea resembles the poet in that it figures both alienation and submission, power and response. Perhaps the clearest placement of the sea in Dickinson's cosmic hierarchy appears in "The Moon is distant from the Sea," a poem that sandwiches ocean between heavenly moon and earthly poet as rival figures for control. The first two stanzas emphasize the Moon's power to lead the Sea, "docile as a Boy," up and down the strand. "He comes just so far," the poem observes, "toward the Town— / Just so far—goes away." The first two stanzas domicile the Sea within the "Amber Hands" of the Moon and the yellow sands of the beach. But, in a typically oblique final stanza, Dickinson upsets her hierarchy by placing a divine "Signior" above the Moon, and the rhythmic Sea also above herself:

> Oh, Signior, Thine, the Amber Hand—
> And mine—the distant Sea—
> Obedient to the least command
> Thine eye impose on me—

The poet submits to commands as the Sea does, and she places her "I" beneath the supernatural "eye" of the Signior.

To submit to heavenly control appears the duty of tidal waters and human souls. The Sea may disrupt and provide an alternative to the rigid ways of the Town, but it also finds a place inside a divinely ordained cosmos. The poet calls the Sea "mine" because she identifies with its obedience as well as with its movement.

Elsewhere Dickinson signals a similar hierarchy in the relationship between rivers and the sea. "My River runs to thee" explores erotic attachment through the hierarchy in which seas absorb rivers without thereby changing their own nature. The oblique early poem of 1861, "Least Rivers," constructs a comparable system in two short lines:

> Least Rivers—docile to some sea.
> My Caspian—thee.

As in "The Moon is distant," Dickinson identifies with the sea but uses that identification to situate herself inside a hierarchy. This pattern appears in several places in her poems. The Sea submits to divine law in the poem "At least—to pray," as Jesus sets "Maelstrom, in the Sea." In "It tossed—and tossed," a poem of shipwreck that resembles "Two swimmers" viewed from the point of view of the ship, the pitiless waters swallow crew and vessel. "The Ocean's Heart," the poem concludes, "too smooth—too Blue— / To Break for You—." Humans submit to Ocean, but even Ocean resides beneath wave-bending powers.

Oceanic Vision

The sea Emily Dickinson sees from her inland home in Amherst erupts into view through the force of imaginative discovery. She writes as mythic explorer, charting alien vistas. The defining characteristic of her ocean, which combines its anti-terrestrial lure and more-than-human hierarchies, presses into the reader with ecstatic force. Of the many sea poems that haunt my daily swims and reveries, none takes me offshore with more urgency than her two-stanza lyric that begins:

> Exultation is the going
> Of an inland soul to sea—
> Past the Houses—
> Past the Headlands—
> Into deep Eternity—

Inside the transformative word "Exultation" the poet's longing for a different world strains itself open. The "inland soul" journeys into Ocean through undifferentiated "going," an abstraction that captures movement from known to unknown, domestic to global spaces. The accoutrements of human life, man-made "Houses" and natural "Headlands," fall away so that the great waters become the image and reality of "deep Eternity." No opening stanza in Dickinson sweeps me forward with the same velocity. I recite this stanza to myself when I dive into the chilly gray-green waters of Long Island Sound each spring, after a long winter in indoor pools.

She never leaves us in simple exultation, and seldom enough in anything like placid "Eternity." The second stanza complicates, bends our neck back to gaze at the disappearing shoreline:

> Bred as we, among the mountains,
> Can the sailor understand
> The divine intoxication
> Of the first league out from Land?

Swimming out but now accompanied by an oddly mountain-bred sailor, a hybrid figure combining land and sea, "we" scan the horizon both ways, with the rhyming pair of "understand" and "Land" framing the poem's mountains-to-sea oscillation. The second stanza's "divine intoxication" redoubles the opening "exultation," but with new emphasis on human weakness. Poet and sailor pass "out from Land" into vastness and incomprehension. I feel that dislocation on my suddenly cold skin each spring when I dive off a granite outcrop into saltwater at high tide.

The visionary sea that I find most intensely in "Exultation is the going" also limns the imaginative force of the sea elsewhere in Dickinson's poetry. In "There is no Frigate like a book," another simple-seeming poem whose title has entered the Hallmark lexicon, the journey of "prancing

Poetry" undergirds the ship's oceanic progress. In "I many times thought Peace had come," the poet identifies with shipwrecked sailors who "deem they sight the Land— / At Centre of the Sea—." The wartime poet's vision of peace in this poem of 1863 is as "fictitious" as the safety the "Wrecked Men" do not really glimpse. The home these abandoned figures imagine in the heart of the sea mirrors the unsettling imaginative waterscape of Dickinson's poetry.

An early lyric of 1858 clarifies the relationship between a ship going to sea and the poet writing a poem. "Whether my bark went down at sea" juxtaposes shipwreck with voyages to "isles enchanted." The poet-ship ventures out, and her capacity for vision frames the voyage:

> By what mystic mooring
> She is held today—
> This is the errand of the eye
> Out upon the Bay.

Moored by a "mystic" connection to the water in language that anticipates the erotic vision of "Wild nights," the poet-ship "is held" in an alien environment. The artist's task or "errand of the eye" re-sees the Oceanic no-place as a vision of partial hospitality, of "exultation" and discovery. The errand of that eye-I captures the essentially speculative nature of the human relationship with the great waters. As Dickinson's lyrics show, the Sea helps us think—differently.

It's possible to interpret Emily Dickinson's fascination with the sea in two distinct but complementary ways. She wrote in nineteenth-century America, and her era witnessed the most dramatic increase in ocean-borne travel in human history. Like Herman Melville, Lord Byron, and Jane Austen, she registered the rise of transoceanic shipping in her art. Like many other poets of the Romantic era, she found in the inhuman vastness of the Sea both an apt metaphor for the transcendent imagination and a technical challenge for lyric poignancy. The Sea became the world during Romanticism. It's a Core story for her also.

But I also think that Dickinson loved the sea for everything it was not: not Amherst, not human, not present to her daily labors. Its Alien waters confronted her at every turn with counterpoint, opposition, inaccessibility. I like to think that poetic art gets made through the encounter of ambition and impossibility. Her Sea was World and also Negation, presence and absence both. Alien and Core together. I value Dickinson's oceanic poetry as environmental art, describing the mismatches and half-glimpses through which humans live in our more-than-human world.

But I'm the sort of person who murmurs lines of Dickinson's poetry to himself every spring when I dive for the first time into too-cold saltwater.

9 MYTH II: QUEEQUEG AND OTHER MERMAIDS

Romantic sea fever followed European maritime empires around the globe during the nineteenth century. Visions of human intimacy with the ocean faced off against snowy Alpine peaks as the essential vistas of the Romantic sublime. Keats' "eternal whisperings" and "mighty swell" ("The Sea") associated the marine with human longings, and Tennyson's "Crossing the Bar" made mortality itself assume oceanic shape, with Death arriving as "a tide that moving seems asleep, / Too full for sound and foam." Lurking behind these portraits of the human-ocean encounter was the fantasy of a truly marine human, a fish-man who could be at home in the waves. The Ovidian figure of Glaucus, a mortal fisherman who became a sea-god after eating a magical herb, becomes in William Diaper's piscatorial *Nereides, or Sea-Eclogues* (1712) a poetic representation of marine utopia, "Where unmixt Waters are as Chrystal clear." Mermaids, sirens, selkies, and other half-human oceanic creatures were already familiar figures in ancient and early modern folklore and mythology—Columbus claimed to have sighted mermaids off Hispaniola in 1493—but the surge in literacy and popular print culture increased the visibility of these figures in the nineteenth century. The celebrated Hans Christian Andersen fable, *The Little Mermaid* (1837), presents a paradigmatic nineteenth-century love-tragedy underwritten by the desire to merge humans with the sea. The tale of the mermaid princess who loves a human prince enough to lose her tongue and walk on knives propels itself through the alien lure of the oceanic world. Popular stories about mermaids, from Oscar Wilde's "The Fisherman and His Soul" (1891) to H. G. Wells' *The Sea Lady* (1902), and Edith Nesbit's *Wet Magic* (1913), reveal the continuing currency of a fantasy that would arrive in comic-book form with D.C.'s *Aquaman* in 1941, and on Hollywood's big screen in James Wan's $200-million-dollar blockbuster, *Aquaman*, starring Jason Mamoa, which opened in the United States the week I drafted this chapter.

No mermaid of any era seems more aquatic or alluring than Queequeg, the cannibal hero who joins narrator Ishmael to sail the world's oceans in Herman Melville's *Moby-Dick*. The bond between Queequeg and Ishmael captures the alien flavor of the human passion for the sea. When Ishmael calls his cannibal friend a pagan, we might substitute the word "oceanic." "I'll try a pagan friend," Ishmael muses, "since Christian kindness has proved but hollow courtesy."

Queequeg the mermaid guides Ishmael into oceanic generosity and not-only-human vastness of vision.

Queequeg and the Little Mermaid make an odd pair, with his bald head against her flowing hair and her fish's tail alongside his indecipherable tattoos. They have more in common than may appear at first. Both figures are other-worldly and oceanic, both rescue lost sailors, and both relate to particular human beings through a radicalized version of married love—homoerotic in Queequeg's case, and silent in the Mermaid's. For Melville and Andersen, these figures balance on the oceanic cusp, luring human swimmers just a bit farther into the deep water than we can abide. The Mermaid and the cannibal draw human love for the ocean out to the edge of human capacities. We love these figures, and they love us, because they dive deeper than we can. These not-only-humans bring us into the water, for as long as we can endure it.

Because We Need to Be Rescued

I've made the point before, when writing about maritime literature, that Queequeg is Melville's Aquaman. He's a rescuer and life buoy, scooping a greenhorn out of the Nantucket drink and later saving Tashtego from drowning inside the sperm whale's capacious head. The "sea Prince of Wales" also saves

Ishmael himself, guiding him onto the *Pequod* and, by means of his custom-built coffin, preserving him alone after the whaleship sinks. In having described Queequeg as Melville's effort to portray a "way of living in intimate contact with the more than human sea," I speculated that the Kokovokan Aquaman represents a principle of oceanic engagement, a way to rescue terrestrial humans and rebirth them into oceanic connection.

The Little Mermaid also comes from an alien space, "Far out in the ocean, where the water is as blue as the prettiest cornflower." She rescues the shipwrecked prince, but unlike Queequeg cannot rove freely with her love around the watery world. Her access to humanity comes at the price of her cut-out tongue and the knives on which she walks in her transformed state. The "bones of shipwrecked human beings" from which the sea hag fashions her house capture the mortal cost of transgressing the oceanic boundary. The Little Mermaid's mute adoration of the prince provides an inverse mirror of the "sea fever" about which nineteenth-century poets rhapsodized, with the crucial difference being that the Mermaid cannot return to her native environment. She's in too deep when she steps out of the surf.

Entangling the stories of Andersen's and Melville's mermaids emphasizes the erotic nature of oceanic desire. Half-human and half-aquatic, both the Mermaid and Queequeg bridge worlds. They bring us to places we want to go, but fear we can't. That fear speaks of an animal knowledge, a terrestrial revulsion to the unstable sea. Neither mermaid nor cannibal can take us all the way there.

A Marriage with Only One Soul

Andersen's fable about the lonely mermaid contains an allegory about bodies and souls. In desiring the prince, the youngest of the five mermaid daughters, whose "skin was as clear and delicate as a rose-leaf, and eyes as blue as the deepest sea," craves what she lacks: a human soul. Gaining a soul comes only through heteronormative marriage in the painful logic of the fable. "Unless a man were to love you so much that you were more to him than his father or mother," cautions the Mermaid's grandmother, "and if all his thoughts and all his love were fixed upon you . . . then his soul would glide into your body and you would obtain a share in the future happiness of mankind." The image of male soul entering the mermaid's half-fishy body eroticizes the spiritual, making the soul she seeks a partial analogy to sexuality, to pregnancy, or perhaps to a materialist understanding of Christian communion. To be souled, for the Mermaid, means leaving the water.

His pagan obeisance to the idol Yojo may not obliterate Queequeg's immortal soul, but clearly what catches Ishmael's attention is all body. "You cannot hide the soul," he observes, but in describing his cannibal friend he lingers on Queequeg's outside, from his "unearthly tattooings" to "his large, deep eyes, fiery black and bold." Finding the cannibal's head to be "phrenologically an excellent one," he concludes that Queequeg must be "George Washington cannibalistically developed." Even at their first meeting, when the pair are thrust into bed together at the Spouter Inn, Queequeg appears "a clean, comely looking cannibal." After the pair meet, Ishmael reports that, "I turned in, and never slept better in my life." Describing Queequeg as "a creature in the transition state—neither caterpillar nor butterfly" enables Ishmael to position his bedmate adjacent to humanity, in much the in-between state of the transformed Little Mermaid. Even Queequeg's pidgin "Who-e debel you?" language finds a partial echo in the mute silence of the transformed Mermaid who loses her tongue to the sea hag's knife. Both of the semi-human figures engage their beloved humans alongside the sea. Both humans, Ishmael and the prince, owe their lives to their mermaid loves.

A Marriage That Leads Only One Way

After going down with the ship, Queequeg symbolically rises, at novel's end, as the coffin-life buoy that preserves Ishmael alone. The Little Mermaid vanishes into sea-foam and eventually sails up to become one of the "daughters of the air." The implications are clear: marriages to oceanic creatures cannot last in this world.

The harpooneer's intimacy with death during his illness transforms him from Ishmael's "fast bosom-friend" into an emissary of the supernatural. Fever causes Queequeg's eyes to grow "fuller and fuller; they became of a strange softness and lustre; and mildly but deeply looked out at you there from his sickness, a wondrous testimony to that immortal health in him which would not die, or be weakened." As the crew remarks on his stoicism—"Queequeg dies game!" quips Pip, and Starbuck lauds his death-induced wisdom— the cannibal at last returns to life to perform "a little duty ashore." Queequeg asserts his power over death, that "if a man make up his mind to live, mere sickness could not kill him." Copying the designs of his tattoos onto the coffin that will later save Ishmael, Queequeg spans the human and divine worlds. Perhaps only Ahab glimpses the true meaning of Queequeg's body: "Oh, devilish tantalization of the gods," the Captain says when failing to decipher his intricate tattoos. Love of Queequeg guides Ishmael to the doomed ship, and the last burst into the air of the coffin-life buoy preserves him in the wake of the disaster.

The Little Mermaid also marries death, or nearly so. Having lost her tongue, she cannot speak or sing to the prince, who chooses to marry a human princess rather than the mute child the mermaid has become. Andersen's story focuses on the experience of the mermaid's last instants in her body: "The sun rose above the waves, and his warm rays fell on the cold foam of the little mermaid, who did not feel as if she were dying." Instead of cold sea-foam, she becomes a spirit of the air, opening a path for a sequel to the fable that was never written. The Little Mermaid's partial death and Queequeg's time in his coffin preserve the prince and

Ishmael from mortal loss while also inviting readers to glimpse beyond the veil. These magical brides court and deflect death's touch.

Two Kinds of Labor

When Ishmael holds Queequeg by the monkey-rope as the cannibal-mermaid balances on a slain whale's back amid a sea of snapping sharks, the harpooneer's body "appeared to uncommon advantage." When the Little Mermaid rescues the shipwrecked prince and carries his unconscious body to shore, "he seemed to her like the marble statue from her garden, and she kissed him again, and wished that he might live." One kind of labor watches from aboard ship, tied fast to the water-creature, Ishmael's "individuality now merged in a joint-stock company of two." The other receives from the prince she rescues "no smile; he knew not that she had saved him." A lifeline to the ship above and an aquatic support from below: these are the kinds of supporting labor human bodies need to survive the oceanic encounter.

For both Melville and Andersen, the perilous connection between mortals and semi-oceanic creatures shows itself in erotic terms. Ishmael observes that he and Queequeg "were wedded" by the monkey-rope and its "elongated Siamese ligature." The Little Mermaid's love for the handsome human grows as the sun "brought back the hue of health to the prince's cheeks," though he does not open his eyes until the young human girl who will be his future bride awakens him. The Little Mermaid returns to the undersea world but dwells in sadness: "she gave up tending her flowers, and they grew in wild confusion on the paths, twining their long leaves and stems round the branches of the trees, so the whole place became dark and gloomy." From this death-sea she will rise to her own destruction, as she had to the prince's preservation. Like Queequeg, the mermaid protects her beloved at the cost of her own life.

Why We Love the Unknown

"Upon waking the next morning about daylight," Ishmael observes, "I found Queequeg's arm thrown over me in the most loving and affectionate manner." In this moment of unconscious domesticity, "you had almost thought I had been his wife." Ishmael's romance with the cannibal harpooneer amounts to bringing an alien presence into his bed, transforming an oceanic soul into a human bond. More than the African Daggoo or Native American Tashtego, Queequeg from the South Seas represents harpooneer as emissary from the unknown. As Ishmael observes about Queequeg's mysterious home island of Kokovoko, "It is not down in any map; true places never are." When the cannibal left home, an American whaleship at first "spurned his suit" to join the crew, requiring eager Queequeg to board without permission and labor before the mast to earn his passage to the wide seas. The love Ishmael feels for Queequeg parallels the narrator's affection for "my dear Pacific . . . [which] zones the world's whole bulk about." The chapter that first places Queequeg in his coffin gets followed immediately by Ishmael's rhapsody to the Pacific: the talismanic cannibal teaches the oceanic wisdom that Ishmael will later transfer from lost Queequeg to the wider seas.

Despite being a children's fable, *The Little Mermaid* too defines itself through the urge to explore. Even before she sees the prince, the youngest daughter wishes to travel to the world above: "Nothing gave her so much pleasure as to hear of the world above the sea." A creature in transition, like Queequeg, the mermaid sacrifices herself to span land and ocean. That urge toward the alien element defines Romanticism's affinity for the ocean. To writers like Andersen, Melville, and many others, the bitter taste of saltwater represents the real, alluring, and painful truth of the world beyond the human.

10 WET GLOBALIZA-
TION II: CONTAINERS

From wombs to coffins, human bodies need containers. We fear to encounter the world's seas alone. The history of human entanglements with watery environments traces itself as a history of the vessels that contain us.

The three crucial containers in this brief history of the human experience of the World Ocean will be the sailing ship, the slave ship, and one particular metal box in a recycling center in Brooklyn inside of which I saw a performance of *Macbeth* in October 2018. These three vessels sketch the narrative of compression, suffering, and tragic focus that defines human modernity's encounter with the great waters. The theoretical frame into which I pour these three ship structures—the container around these containers—comes via the German philosopher Peter Sloterdijk's monumental project of "spherology," as elaborated across the three substantial volumes of *Spheres* (1998–2003). In the first volume of the trilogy, *Bubbles: Spheres I* (German 1998, English 2011), Sloterdijk argues that human selves only develop by seeking out containment and the temporary stability it produces. Opening with a stunning reading of a child contemplating a soap bubble, Sloterdijk asserts that "all things belonging to the world or being as a whole [. . .] [are] to be contained in a breath like an indelible purpose." Like soap bubbles, all containers eventually break. Moments of rupture represent transitions: "All amniotic sacs, organic models of autogenous vessels, live towards their bursting; with the turbulent waters of birth, every life is washed up on the coast of harder facts." The emblematic rupture of the womb develops across Sloterdijk's expansive project into a "*general theory of autogenous vessels*" that extends from bubbles to "globes" during the early modern period of transoceanic globalization into the more chaotic "foams" of the postmodern present. Human history and psychology both strain against and take comfort in residing within sphere-shaped bubbles, globes, and foams. In this model, to live is to be contained.

Sloterdijk's abstract spheres may seem distant from the labor and camaraderie fostered by sailing ships. But Joseph Conrad's career-long hymn to the community of maritime labor gestures toward a comparable enfolding of intimacy through skilled work. Margaret Cohen argues in *The Novel and the Sea* (2010) that Conrad's sea stories write a sustained elegy for the seaman's craft and the solidarities that craft creates. In *The Mirror of the Sea*, Conrad insists that the vessel takes priority even over the sailors. "After all," he writes, "the art of handling ships is finer, perhaps, than the art of handling men." The repetitive pressure of the word *art* in Conrad's prose insists that he's metaphorically talking about writing, and that he sees his artistic task as ship-contained more than simply human-directed. The ship-as-artwork protects fragile men who venture onto the common grave and opacity of the ocean. When Conrad sounds his Romantic ocean-theme, he emphasizes violence and terror:

> As if it were too great, too mighty for common virtues, the ocean has no compassion, no faith, no law, no memory. Its fickleness is to be held true to men's purposes only by an undaunted resolution and by a sleepless, armed, jealous vigilance, in which, perhaps, there has always been more hate than love.

At the center of this description of oceanic ambivalence sits an image of containing—"to be held true"—in which human hands somehow embrace the fullness of ocean. That holding, the sailing-man's craft and community, sometimes and to some degree protects human bodies from salty alien depths. In the practice of "that skill which passes into art" sailors and ships form temporary Sloterdijkian spheres.

The sustaining force of these containing spheres never quite monumentalizes itself, either in Conrad's prose or in the long history of navigation. Storms and shipwrecks, those essential features of maritime literature, represent glimpses into the maelstrom from a fragile and only marginally safe space. "If you would know the age of the earth," intones

Conrad, "look upon the sea in a storm." To encounter this reality tests craft and community, and the result, if it is not catastrophe, produces global maritime connections, and sometimes also transcendent visionary art:

> To see, to see!—This is the craving of the sailor, as of the rest of blind humanity.

In the English pun between *see* and *sea*, non-native speaker Conrad defines his most lofty ambitions. The sailor knows the sea through what Conrad calls the "machinery" of tackle, sails, spars, and arcane terms. Through the human communities assembled in and by these machines, whose displacement by steam and then diesel vessels comprises the central lament of Conrad's career, bubbles form, float, and eventually break. Seeing and working inside sailing bubbles carves out human spaces in oceanic immensity.

Conrad's idealization of the sailing ship dovetails with familiar evocations of the ship as state, as self, or as a vessel for heroic exploration, from the voyages of Captain James Cook to those of Captain James Kirk. But that imperialist and masculinist vision, which Conrad only partly ironizes, occludes what happens below decks. The central human tragedy in Western oceanic modernity, as noted earlier, was the Middle Passage. The forced transportation of over twelve million Africans to the Americas between 1525 and 1866 reshaped both the Old and New Worlds, created hybrid creole cultures in the Western hemisphere, and directly caused the death of nearly two million Africans en route. The slave ship, not the Romantic clipper ship, birthed the modern world. This horrific event carried its human cargo in vessels that Marcus Rediker describes as "a strange combination of war machine, mobile prison, and factory." Any comprehension of the human relationship with oceanic movement needs to reckon with human cargo below decks.

An essential witness of the Middle Passage, as I've previously noted, is Olaudah Equiano, who carefully registers the deadly containing vessel as hostile environment:

> The stench of the hold while we were on the coast was so intolerably loathsome, that it was dangerous to remain there for any time . . . but now that the whole ship's cargo were confined together, it became absolutely pestilential.

Equiano describes the hold of the slave ship in terms that recast Sloterdijk's bubbles into places of violent compression. Further elaborating the experience of the hold leads Édouard Glissant to a brutal vision of containment as mortality:

> Imagine two hundred human beings crammed into a space barely capable of containing a third of them. Imagine vomit, naked flesh, swarming lice, the dead slumped, the dying crouched.

Humans consigned to the dark hold invert the fluttering visibility of Conrad's sailors working aloft. The slave ship, which historian Stephanie Smallwood cogently describes as "a place of unparalleled displacement," ruptured and recreated the lives of transported Africans. As Rediker describes the historical process, these ships created a new people: "At the beginning of the Middle Passage, captains loaded on board the vessel a multiethnic collection of Africans, who would, in the American port, become 'black people' or a 'negro race.'" Within the hold, mostly in darkness, surrounded by death, modernity birthed itself.

Treating the slave ship as driver of the modern project recasts the dreams of even self-aware imperialists. The colonialist hypocrisy of figures such as Conrad has been well-exposed by postcolonial critics and writers such as Chinua Achebe. The creative pressure that emerges from the slave ship, however, has not yet been given as much cultural attention as the iconic symbol of the clipper ship under sail. If the sailing ship represents political order from *Moby-Dick* to the yachting literature epitomized by Joshua Slocum's *Sailing Alone Around the World* (1900), the Middle Passage produced an oppositional idea of freedom out of the maroon's conditions of extremity. Returning to Neil Roberts' *Freedom as Marronage*, the rejection of slavery creates not a temporary escape but a permanent condition: "Freedom is not a place; it is a state of being." Claiming that this stance, built in and through hybrid societies in the New World, is not "anti-Western but post-Western," Roberts generates a positive alternative to the familiar genealogy of Western discourses of freedom and politics. Seeking "acts of flight that are at moments evanescent, dialectic, [and] overlapping," marronage becomes a political and cultural strategy for building a New World on the far side of the Atlantic.

These two vessels—the death-pregnant holds of slavers, and the swelling white canvas of clipper ships—divide conceptions of oceanic modernity over the past half-millennium. In a physical sense, however, the rectangular metal containers that first appeared in American ports in the late 1950s and now populate every major cargo port on the globe have overtaken both maritime vessels as symbols of postmodern globalization. Containers carry the mercantile cargo that clipper ships once hauled, and they also smuggle human cargoes of refugees in a modern redistribution of the Middle Passage. Ocean now floats in a steel box. The shipping container is the dominant contemporary form of the intimate environment that Sloterdijk theorized through the image of the sphere. The consequences for art, commerce, and the oceanic imagination are still being written.

In the fall of 2018 I caught an oblique glimpse of what containerized art might become.

I showed up at the Sure We Can recycling center in Bushwick about twenty minutes before the show was supposed to start. I was not sure I was in the right place. An open door guided me off the sidewalk into a maze of stacked pallets and aluminum cans stuffed to bursting in clear plastic bags. I didn't see anyone who looked as if they were going to the theatre,

but the space was intriguingly speckled with colorful graf-
fiti, so I wandered around in the lingering twilight. Someone
found me and asked, "Are you here for Makbet?" He thread-
ed me through the maze to an opening that contained a fire
burning in a half-sized oil drum, around which the members
of the company were gathered. One member of the group,
after checking her phone, addressed me by name. I pleaded
vegetarianism when they offered kielbasa wrapped in news-
paper but accepted a small glass of vodka. Mostly the people
around the fire were actors; clearly the container would not
be full on a chilly October night.

The rules of the game for Makbet-in-the-box orchestrated
multiple roles through costumes: a black hat for Makbet, red
shawl for his Lady, berets for Banquo and Fleance, spectacles
for Prince Malcolm, a bandanna for Macduff. The royal trench
coat would be worn in succession by the three kings of Scotland:
Duncan, Makbet, and finally Malcolm. Three members of the
company passed the props around as they exchanged the roles.
Three Makbets raged and killed and rhapsodized inside the
narrow metal box—one speculative and focused on the air-
drawn dagger; a second manic and expressive; a third intense
and withdrawn, especially when wearing the monarchal coat.
Watching the actors pass the roles around intensified the play's
recursive focus on ambition, violence, loss, and the lure of
visionary knowledge. I've seen a lot of good productions of this
play, but none quite like this one.

Working with a compressed script in a compressed space,
taking advantage of the narrow steel walls for sound and

mood, the company generated a powerfully claustrophobic version of Shakespeare's dark tragedy. I loved the abrupt turns of the role-switching. And I loved that it all fit inside the box. Container art may be the Anthropocene future of oceanic art.

After the tyrant's death, with the final battle punctuated by the crash of human bodies against steel walls, the trio ritually repacked the costume props inside a large stainless steel lobster pot. They held hands in a ring. "Peace," each said to the next. "Peace," to me where I sat on a hard wooden bench. "Peace." Then—smash!—the steel lid slammed down on the pot. "The charm's wound up!" And reality flooded back, flickering with incandescent lights.

I had a long drive home, so I lingered only for a minute around the fire to break bread with the company. But I left thinking that all plays should be performed in narrow, chilly, dark steel containers. Because inside those boxes we make our world.

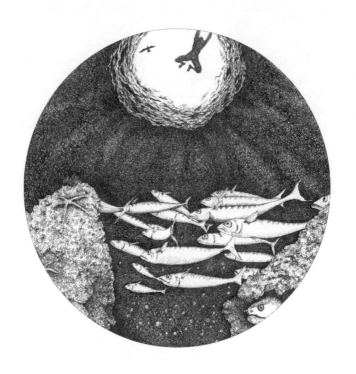

11 BLUE ENVIRON-MENTALISM: RACHEL CARSON

The Mountain rears himself high, aloof, and majestic. He sees and knows. Nothing is alien to the Mountain because everything lies under his gaze. We who live beneath the Mountain await his opaque commands. His voice may yet repeal large codes of fraud and woe, because from his cloud-rimmed vantage point we are all the same, all connected, all miniscule.

The Mountain's song rings out in many voices, from Percy Shelley to John Muir, but his clearest spokesman for modern American environmentalists is Aldo Leopold.

The Sea spreads and reaches every side, angling her fingers up and down each coastal plain. She feels and touches. She is alien to we who live on land, but in her bitter salt we taste an ancient intimacy. We love and fear and do not understand her. Her murmurs trouble our dreams and freeze our tongues. She gnaws the shoreline as the cold hard mouth of the world, to which all chasms must open at last. The Sea connects and estranges, buoys and drowns, fascinates and repels.

This book has sung many Sea-songs, but no singer touches closer to the heart of the matter than the poet-scientist of the tide pools, Rachel Carson. Her blue environmentalism counterflows Leopold's Mountain-thinking. She reminds us that the Ocean, in time, will dissolve the Mountain. In that dissolution lies a blue environmental future.

"In the sea," Carson wrote in her first book, the reception of which was smothered in the wartime fervor of 1941, "nothing is lost." *Under the Sea-Wind* represents Carson's emerging voice, including her recognition that "the sea itself must be the central character" in her writing. By entering into the voices of three maritime creatures—the gull, Rynchops; the mackerel, Scomber; and the eel, Anguilla—Carson anthropomorphizes herself and her readers into three different modes of oceanic experience. The gull observes tides and the sea's changes, feeding himself from its bounty. The mackerel swims between deep and shallow marine environments. The eel, smallest but most dramatic, transitions from maturity in freshwater rivers to spawning grounds in the deep Atlantic. All three creatures attune themselves to the ocean's rhythms and forces. Humans, when they appear in Carson's narrative, usually interrupt natural spaces, as in the case of the "strange disturbance" that is the trawl net:

It was like nothing [the mackerel] had experienced in their life in the harbor, nor during that earlier period, now only the dimmest of memories, when they had drifted with the other plankton at the surface of the sea. It came to them as a heavy, thudding vibration felt with the lateral-line canals over their sensitive flanks. It was not the feel of water vibrations over a rocky reef, nor of waves on a tide rip—yet these sensations were perhaps the nearest akin to it of anything the young mackerel had known.

The sinister arrival of the trawl, "something vast and dark, like a fish of monstrous and incredible size," violates Carson's undersea utopia. Writing before the crash of fish-stocks in the late twentieth century, she proleptically recognizes the destructive force of industrial fishing methods. The "vast, gaping mouth" of the trawl net represents the ocean's cruel human future.

The story of environmental degradation at which Carson would arrive two decades later in *Silent Spring*, however, did not overwrite her earliest work. Instead, *Under the Sea-Wind* concludes with a scientist's turn toward inhuman temporalities and the long conflict between erosive sea and assertive mountains. Although Leopold's iconic "Thinking Like a Mountain" essay would not be published for another seven years, the final image of Carson's first book anticipates the conflict between sea and stone. "The sea, too," she writes, "lay restless, awaiting the time when once more it should encroach upon the coastal plain." She places this tension in geologic context:

[S]o the relation of sea and coast and mountain ranges was that of a moment in geologic time. For once more the mountains would be worn away by the endless erosion of water and carried in silt to the sea, and once more all the coast would be water again, and the places of its cities and towns would belong to the sea.

In an age of rising sea levels and coastal superstorms, Carson's words now carry a hint of urgent destruction that may not have occurred to her earliest readers in the 1940s. Her vision of a mountain-eating ocean that swamps coastal dwellings may now be transforming itself into the reality of human as well as geologic time.

Aldo Leopold's *A Sand County Almanac*, published posthumously in 1948, sits at the heart of twentieth-century American environmentalism. Along with the works of John Muir and the inspiration many writers and activists take from Henry David Thoreau, Leopold's hymn to the sustaining power of "wild things" suffuses popular ideas about the value of wilderness and land conservation. The Thoreau-Muir romance of the American West helped support the politics that founded the National Park system. As ecofeminist scholar Catriona Sandilands has noted, however, these men's vision of the value of wild places built itself atop racist and sexist ideas about the masculine need to escape feminized domestic space and to separate themselves from growing urban and immigrant populations. Sandilands and others who imagine queer ecologies and queer environments ask that we reconsider the wild outside the monolithic masculinity of its influential champions. Leopold's mountain-thinking bears reexamination in light of both Carson's oceanic alternative and Sandilands' queer ecology.

At the core of Leopold's environmentalism is what he calls a "land ethic" that envisions all the inhabitants of an ecosystem in mutual community. He fixes on the mountain as the symbol of that community because "Only the mountain has lived long enough." Only the mountain, Leopold surmises, has the perspective and distance necessary to see the environment as a whole. This powerful image invests the physical qualities of the mountain with insight and power. The mountain's features—immense height, solitude, immobility, impassive silence—represent knowledge. Leopold's vision of ecosystemic totality itself remains relatively bounded; he does not consider geologic time spans over the course of which mountains themselves flow, move, and erode. As Jeffrey Jerome Cohen observes in *Stone: An Inhuman Ecology* (2015), even rocks, the most inanimate of objects, evince liveliness and desire, given the right geological or poetic perspectives.

Leopold recognized the environmentalist's task as one of moral development, and he explicitly constructs the land ethic as part of an "ethical sequence." His counterexample, interestingly, is the sailor Odysseus, who, after he arrives home from his wanderings, hangs the enslaved women who have been sleeping with the suitors in Ithaca. According to Leopold, Odysseus did not hesitate to execute the slaves because he owned them: "The disposal of property was then, as now, a matter of expediency, not of right or wrong." Leopold extends his metaphor by noting that in the mid-twentieth century, "Land, like Odysseus' slave-girls, is still property." Leopold aims to change a purely instrumental understanding of the land into a sympathetic one. He may, however, have oversimplified Homer's presentation of the killing of the enslaved women. Telemachus, not Odysseus, performs the execution. The poem notes that the son's idea to hang the slaves represents his own "initiative," not his father's judgment. The slaves' deaths become an occasion for tragic pathos, not simple justice:

As doves or thrushes spread their wings to fly
home to their nests, but someone sets a trap—
they crash into a net, a bitter bedtime;
just so the girls, their heads all in a row;
were strung up with the noose around their necks
to make their death an agony. They gasped,
feet twitching for a while, but not for long.

As the poem's most recent and first female translator, Emily Wilson, has observed, the history of published translations of this passage has long included a series of slurs against the enslaved women as "sluts" or "whores," neither of which accusations seems merited by the Greek text. As her version makes clear, these deaths are morally dubious, rather than a matter of the neutral disposal of property. Perhaps Homer was farther along the ethical sequence than Leopold realized.

In the two volumes published in the 1950s, *The Sea Around Us* (1951) and *The Edge of the Sea* (1955), Carson completed her sea trilogy by expanding her vision as both scientist and poet. The first of these two volumes begins with the "shadowy . . . beginnings of that great mother of life, the sea." Carson tells of endless ocean-filling rains after the hardening of the planet's crust and the tearing away of a massive layer of granite to become the moon, leaving behind a depression that now forms the Pacific basin. Her story differs slightly from my Alien or Core narration of Ocean's origins, in part because of changes in geological theories over the past seventy years. But the tension she observes between dissolving saltwater and eroding rock remains the essential contrapuntal narrative of land and sea:

> It is an endless, inexorable process that has never stopped—the dissolving of the rocks, the leaching out of their contained minerals, the carrying of the rock fragments and dissolved minerals to the ocean. And over the eons of time, the sea has grown ever more bitter with the salt of the continents.

None of the many subjects Carson touches in *The Sea Around Us* gives rise to more resonant poetry than ocean sediments. She describes the sinking of biotic materials from dead microbes and other living creatures as a "long snowfall." "The sediments" that fall, she writes, "are a sort of epic poem of the earth." Falling into the deep ocean as if into endless history, ocean sediments represent an archive of natural processes, "the outpouring of volcanoes, the advance and retreat of the ice, the searing aridity of desert lands, the sweeping destruction of floods." In the vertical dimension, Ocean records planetary history.

Within her breakout success *The Sea Around Us* hide the seeds of the focus that would distinguish the last of Carson's sea books. Writing in the middle volume that "the boundary between sea and land is the most fleeting and transitory feature of the earth," Carson foreshadows the wet margins that would become the center of *The Edge of the Sea*. Revealing herself to be tide-pool gatherer more than ocean swimmer, her third and final sea volume isolates "an area of unrest where waves have broken heavily against the land." The impermanence of the seashore defines its attraction: "For no two successive days is the shore line precisely the same." After a long ramble along rocky, marshy, and sandy shores, she arrives at "the unifying touch of the sea" as marker of sameness and difference. On the salty edge, Carson's poetic voice anticipates by half a century the visionary intermingled human and nonhuman ecopoetics of twenty-first-century thinkers, including Jane Bennett, Donna Haraway, Stacy Alaimo, and Bruno Latour. Her sea is Alien and Core, a no-place "in which there is no finality, no ultimate and fixed reality—earth becoming fluid as the sea itself." She poises her voice on the cusp of sea and land and balances in that precarious and vanishing place. The murmuring sea-voice almost whispers to her, or rather it whispers and she can almost imagine she understands, that the tide on her toes proffers "an uneasy sense of the communication of some universal truth that lies just beyond our grasp." That's where I like to leave Carson in my imagination: with wet feet, on the beach, listening to the dying echoes of retreating waves.

That's not where environmental history usually places Carson, because although *The Edge of the Sea* was the last volume of her sea trilogy, her most influential and least oceanic book, *Silent Spring*, appeared seven years later in 1962. The pastoral vision of small-town America that opens her exposé of the evils of DDT powerfully choreographs a green utopia:

> There was once a town in the heart of America where all life seemed to live in harmony with its surroundings. The town lay in the midst of a checkerboard of prosperous farms, with fields of grain and hillsides of orchards where, in spring, white clouds of blooms drifted above green fields.

Into this suddenly bird-less and song-less paradise the chemical trails of insecticides burn. The ideal "harmony" of Carson's idyll includes agriculture and industry, and the "checkerboard" even suggests a place for human cultures of play. The ambiguously alien ocean, however, remains out of sight in the book's pastoral vision. She has not forgotten the sea entirely—she details the poisoning of oysters and clams among the detriments of chemical pesticides—but her focus has shifted. Like Aldo Leopold, she's attending to terrestrial landscapes and the worlds humans shape with them. Much as I admire the political consequences of *Silent Spring*, which contributed to the banning of DDT, the founding of the Environmental Protection Agency in 1970, and the celebration of the first Earth Day in 1970, my deepest devotion remains for her ocean books, among the eels and mackerel, splashing in opaque and moving tidal pools.

12 SWIMMERS: IMMERSIVE HISTORIES

The images that have preceded these chapters emerge from the wet hand of Vanessa Daws, artist and swimmer. Swimming caps and goggles show the repeated presence of modern bodies in this *Ocean*, sometimes at the center of the images and sometimes at the margins. Between my ocean swimming and hers, this final chapter hazards some ideas about immersion as a way of inhabiting our watery planet in difficult times. Scalar confusion defines the central image of a solitary swimmer in the planet-girdling Ocean. The small human thing appears tiny, but just like the fluid in which it floats, the body is around two-thirds saltwater. We are all bodies of water, observes ecofeminist Astrida Neimanis, who I first met beside the toxic waters of Newtown Creek in Brooklyn in 2018. When we dare to immerse our small bodies in our globe's watery skin, we feel something. Nothing like control or mastery, but rather a physical intuition or connection, a planetary tug, a faint reminder that one's own water-filled flesh also has tides, also responds to the moon's gravitational embrace, also swims in fluid connections atop a nearly spherical rock in the void.

The core insight of swimming shows itself through feeling. Charles Sprawson quotes Australian Olympic champion freestyler Murray Rose:

> The principal quality . . . demanded of a swimmer is a "feel for the water." He should use his arms and legs as a fish its fins, and be able to feel the pressure of the water on his hands, to hold it in his palm as he pulls the stroke through without allowing it to slip through his fingers.

Sprawson, in his wildly enthusiastic *The Haunts of the Black Masseur: The Swimmer as Hero* (1992), emphasizes the mystical and heroic elements of water-feeling. His swimmer becomes a determined "individualist" who practices a "lonely, meditative" labor that resembles "a continuous dream of a world under water." Sprawson traces sea mysticism from classical poetry to Romantic figures such as Algernon Swinburne, who rhapsodizes that "to feel that in deep water is to feel—as long as one is swimming out . . .—as if one was in another world of life." Sprawson's book idiosyncratically mixes the words of Olympic champions, poets, and his own experiences to pursue the "ichthyosaurus ego" imagined by John Cooper Powys and the immersive figures of "pagan myth" conjured by Rupert Brooke. The "black masseur" of Sprawson's enigmatic title, which reference he never clarifies in the text, alludes to a shockingly racist story by Tennessee

Williams in which a weak white man enters into violent and ultimately destructive erotic communion with a powerful black masseur. The water's touch combines ecstasy with disturbing violence.

When a human body submerges itself in water, we feel disorientation and buoyancy, which transform themselves into resilience and vulnerability. We can't live in water, but we love being in water. Swimmer-writer Leanne Shapton explains that she "feels [her] body acutely in the water." That physical feeling forms a kind of understanding: "It's a knowledge of watery space, being able to sense exactly where my body is and what it's affecting, an animal empathy for contact with an element." James Hamilton-Patterson, an English writer whose passion for water drew him to spend an entire year "liv[ing] alone in the middle of the sea" on an uninhabited island in the Philippines, sees in the "hypocrite swimmer" an image of dissolution: "He only has existed as three-tenths and that fraction is melting into water." Feeling in this context brings physical sensation together with an intuitive grasp of vastness and motion. Swimming means feeling the hyperobject ocean against bare skin. As our Anthropocene environment grows more dynamic and unsettled, the swimmer's practice of partial order amid constant threats may usefully become a dream of partial resilience. As Astrida Neimanis observes, an essential project in our chaotic environment will be to "learn to swim." No better tools for this learning present themselves than our bodies and the world's oceans. I like swim goggles too.

Vanessa Daws practices swimming as meditation, allegory, and being-in-the-world. These reflections respond to her 2016 circumnavigational swim of Lambay Island, the first time anyone had swum around the largest island on the east coast of Ireland:

bubble bubble breath

bubble bubble breath

bubble bubble breath

Every three strokes the head turns with the rotating shoulder and hip, *like pulling back an arrow*. One eye peers out of the water while the other stays below. Salt water slides over goggles, and in the few seconds of incoming breath, two images appear.

In that moment both worlds are visible: above and below the water's skin, divided by a blur of surface reflection. One eye looks down into an immense blue, grey, green, brown body of water. The other sees out above the surface, catching glimpses of far away land, towers, beaches, buildings, bridges, people going about their daily lives, and white crested waves crash over while lungs fill with air.

The swimmer keeps a steady rhythm of breath and moving arms and legs as they journey through the water. That moment is all the swimmer needs to think about. Just one arm in front of the other until they reach land again.

A short practical history of swimming buttresses the dream I share with Vanessa Daws that ocean swimming can become an ecological meditation for the Anthropocene. In the ancient Mediterranean world, as Nicholas Orme notes in his essential history *Early British Swimming* (1983), swimming was a survival practice and military skill, a way of moving armies across rivers and other bodies of water. In Europe, the early modern period saw a flood of new interest in swimming for multiple reasons. Revised translations of ancient and Biblical texts combined with a surge in maritime trade and travel reinvigorated swimming as metaphor and practice. Encounters with African, Native American, and Pacific Islander communities who included strong swimmers impressed European sailors and adventurers, in particular when they were establishing pearl fisheries and other maritime colonial projects.

The central historical text marking the upsurge of interest in swimming in early modern England is Everard Digby's *De Arte Natandi* (1587), a Latin treatise translated into English by Christopher Middleton as *A Short introduction for to learne to Swimme* (1595). In a dedicatory epistle directed to Master Simon Smith, purportedly a good swimmer, Middleton describes swimming as among "commendable exercises tending to profitable ends." Digby's main text emphasizes the value of swimming in "the preserving of man's life" and also "to purge the skin from all external pollutions or uncleanness." The outstanding features of both Digby's and Middleton's books are woodcuts that demonstrate different styles of swimming and aquatic maneuvers. Humans even exceed fish, in Digby's understanding, because of our felicity in "diving down to the bottom of the deepest waters and fetching from thence whatsoever is there sunk down." The swimmer in these pages performs miracles of art and mobility, "sitting, tumbling, leaping, walking," mimicking the features of "a ship at sea," "a dog," and even "a dolphin." Among uniquely human abilities Digby notes our capacity for "'swimming upon the back'—a gift which [Nature] has denied even to the watery inhabitants of the sea." Treating a (male) human body as the measure of all things may be a typical Renaissance affectation, but Digby's intimate portrait of how bodies engage with watery environments gestures toward a growing awareness of swimming as art and experience.

Digby was a Fellow at St. John's College, Cambridge, and the images in his book resemble local aquatic haunts along the

River Cam. While the warm saltwater of the Mediterranean has attracted swimmers since antiquity, recreational ocean swimming in England emerged into popular view only with eighteenth-century ideas about the medicinal shock of cold-water immersion. Alain Corbin has documented the rapid expansion of "the sea bathing fashion . . . out of a therapeutic objective." Not until the turn of the twentieth century and such innovations as the development of underwater photography by Louis Boutan in 1899, the invention of the aqualung by Émile Gagnan and Jacques Cousteau in 1943, and the expansion of surfing and surf culture after World War II did recreational ocean swimming displace medicinal beach going. Global beach tourism in the twentieth century changed the lived relationship between humans and the sea. As sea levels rise and storms powered by global warming attack coastlines in the twenty-first century, our desire to live and play near the shore is coming into conflict with the dynamic instabilities of the Anthropocene.

During Vanessa Daws' three-week stay in Santa Barbara, California, in October 2014, she pursued a "pyschoswimography" or an exploration of a place "through the art of swimming." Interacting with local swimmers including a group that calls itself the "Ocean Ducks" as well as aqua-academics like me at a beach-themed conference, Daws produced a small art book that captures her encounters with California sea-culture and a week of unusually warm Pacific waters. She organized a joint swim during the conference that brought the Ocean Ducks together with enthusiastic conference-go-ers. Stacy Alaimo, a plenary speaker at the conference who swam with us, described the experience:

> It felt like an experiment with becoming a medium for art. To be ourselves in the interchange with the ocean, to be aesthetically overcome by the blues and greens of the water. I won't say the event "elevated" swimming to an art, because elevation would place us above the practice and what is most beautiful to me is to think of how swimming—the immersion of the human in water—releases us from transcendent perspectives, unmoors us as terrestrial creatures, allows us to hover in other ways of being that are, perhaps, less separate from the substances of the world.

I also wrote a short note for *Psychoswimography: Santa Barbara*:

> When land mammals enter the ocean, buoyancy makes things possible. Swimming is flying, almost, and I love its singular touch. But what I remember most about Santa Barbara is the second thing: how artistic practice made swimming into community. We were surrounded by swimmers, Ocean Ducks, surfers, scholars of premodern literature and critical theory, all together in the ocean. To be in that translucent alien world but not alone in it: the gift of art.

For Daws, the essential elements of those days of Pacific immersion were artistic:

> My art explores place through swimming. "Place" being the watery space navigated and swam through, the littoral space surrounding, and the social space created by shared activity.
>
> Chance encounter, swimming, journey, conversation, cups of tea and shivering are the starting points for my art projects, a process I've been describing as "Psychoswimography." The word "swim" added to Psychogeography to shift the meaning from a terrestrial drifting to a watery drifting and re-imagining of place.
>
> Swimming is an activity that connects humans directly to water. A swimmer is "in" this substance of immense power and unknown, swimming is a lived in, embodied experience. Swimming allows us through acclimatization and adaption to surprise ourselves and go beyond our expectations.
>
> But where does this compulsion come from?
>
> This desire to submerge and swim?
>
> Is this urge spiritual, genetic, or social?
>
> Or perhaps it is the sheer thrill of the unknown, to feel the water on our skin, the cold on our head, adapt our breathing and to feel we exist?

Looking back on that October in Santa Barbara, I like to think that we were all part of a collaboration of which swimming was the core, a physical engagement between ocean and human, saltwater and thinking flesh, global fluidity and individual fragments. We were thinking about the ocean, but not only thinking about it. Sometimes even artists and academics need to be overwhelmed.

My talk at the conference in Santa Barbara was about body-surfing. It anticipated the basic duality of this book: thinking and feeling, ideas and immersion, the things we conceptualize and the things we feel on skin.

I brought two mantras from the surf to the lecture hall in California. The first, "Experience is better than knowledge," I borrowed from the early modern French mariner Samuel de Champlain. The second, "Always allegorize!" I adapted from one of the maxims in Fredric Jameson's *The Political Unconscious* (1981). Both translated—or tried to translate— what I feel in the ocean into words.

What I really wanted was both mantras spilling over each other, the overfullness of oceanic experience and the lunging grasp toward intellectual understanding. I wanted the feeling of being in the wave and the comprehension that sometimes flashes out from a well-crafted sentence. To be in the moving ocean and to be thinking about it—both at the same time.

The night after the bodysurfing and the public lecture about bodysurfing, the conference hosted a rooftop party at a swanky Santa Barbara hotel. Many of the people who were there may remember the ruckus caused by an overenthusiastic professor trespassing into the hotel pool. But that's not all I recall from that evening, and not only because I stayed uncharacteristically dry. I remember talking with a poet and labor activist who had heard my bodysurfing talk earlier in the day. "I had never bodysurfed before," she said. "But I went over to Hendry's Beach this afternoon and tried it. I was remembering what you said, about swimming to match the wave's velocity from inside, and I went into the ocean, and—I did it. Caught it. Rode the wave in."

We who try to wedge the great waters into words don't expect it to work all the time. Riding waves is a precarious business, and often you end up with a face full of sand. But sometimes, just for a minute, everything comes together. Experience meets allegory. Human body joins ocean wave. Together these unlike things tumble toward shore.

Feeling the wave won't solve the problems of our rising waters. Allegorizing the ocean won't make Anthropocene dilemmas easier, though the process may surface hidden pleasures and possibilities.

But that feeling and that being, the poetics of swimming and oceanic connection, can punctuate living in our broken environment. It feels good to immerse one's body in the largest thing on the surface of the planet. It teaches a body how to live in this wet world.

ACKNOWLEDGMENTS

Fellow swimmers in the blue humanities have been splashing and thinking together in waters near and far, and this book owes much to the far-flung and speculative community of aqua-academics and water-thinkers. There's no space to sing out all the names, but I'm especially grateful to share this watery current with Stacy Alaimo, Elizabeth Albert, Josiah Blackmore, Dan Brayton, Mary K. Bercaw-Edwards, Jeff Bolster, Hester Blum, Joseph Campana, Siobhan Carroll, Margaret Cohen, Robin Kundis Craig, Lowell Duckert, Marianna Dudley, Hillary Eklund, Ann Elias, Mary Fuller, John Gillis, Sophie Gilmartin, Anne Harris, John Hattendorf, Chris Holmes, Claire Jowitt, Eileen Joy, Richard King, Bernhard Klein, Craig Lambert, Jeffrey McCarthy, Nancy Nowacek, Christopher Pastore, Laurence Publicover, Killian Quigley, Luis Rodríguez Rincón, Martha Elena Rojas, Debapriya Sarkar, James Seth, Phil Steinberg, Dyani Johns Taff, Marina Zurkow, the editors of Underwaternewyork.com, the contributors to Oceanic Bristol and *Oceanic New York*, and many others. This book owes a special debt to Chris Schaberg, Ian Bogost, and Haaris

Naqvi for piloting the good ship *Ocean* through publication with Bloomsbury. Sections of several chapters contain material I delivered as lectures, to the interdisciplinary "Re-Valuing the Ocean" conference at the University of Utah in February 2019: to Harvard University's Department of Romance Languages in March 2019, and the Sydney Environment Institute in October 2019; I benefited from the generosity and feedback of those and other audiences. I'm especially pleased that *Ocean* hosts the visual genius of Vanessa Daws, with whom I've swum and collaborated on Atlantic and Pacific shores.

My three dedicatees have been swimming with me since two of them were born, and I offer this book to them as salty token of love and future adventures.

READING THE BLUE HUMANITIES

Putting the great waters between a small book's covers isn't easy. But that hasn't stopped the sea from sloshing through literary and historical writing for as long as we have written records. This bibliographical essay starts with some suggestions for further oceanic reading, and then goes on to provide sources for this book's quoted materials.

These lists, like their compiler, follow Anglophone and premodern directions. Especially in older historical periods, they tend to be overly male. The lists make no claim for completion or perfect representation. These are the books I know and love and return to obsessively. Open waters beckon.

Ten One-Volume Ocean Histories

1 Jules Michelet, *The Sea*. Katia Stainson, trans. Los Angeles: Green Integer Books, 2012. Orig. French *La mer,* 1861.

2 Joseph Conrad, *The Mirror of the Sea*. New York: Harper and Brothers, 1966. Orig. 1906.

3 Rachel Carson, *The Sea Around Us*. Drawings by Katherine L. Howe. Oxford: Oxford University Press, 1951.

4 J. H. Parry, *The Discovery of the Sea*. New York: Dial Press, 1974.

5 Alain Corbin, *The Lure of the Sea: The Discovery of the Seaside, 1750–1840*. Jocelyn Phelps, trans. New York: Polity Press, 1994. Orig. French 1988.

6 Allan Sekula, *Fish Story*. Düsseldorf: Richter Verlag, 1995.

7 Philip E. Steinberg, *The Social Construction of the Ocean*. Cambridge: Cambridge University Press, 2001.

8 Callum Roberts, *An Unnatural History of the Sea*. Washington: Island Books, 2007.

9 W. Jeffrey Bolster, *The Mortal Sea: Fishing the Atlantic in the Age of Sail*. Cambridge: Harvard University Press, 2012.

10 Helen Rozwadowski, *Vast Expanses: A History of the Oceans*. London: Reaktion, 2018.

Ten Ocean Stories

1 Homer, *The Odyssey* (~8th century BCE)

2 Luís Vaz de Camões, *The Lusiads* (1572)

3 William Shakespeare, *The Tempest* (1611)

4 Daniel Defoe, *Robinson Crusoe* (1719)

Ten Sea Lyrics

Ten Blue Humanities Studies

1 Hester Blum, *The View from the Masthead: Maritime Imagination and Antebellum American Sea Narratives.* Chapel Hill: University of North Carolina Press, 2008.

2 Samuel Baker, *Written on the Water: British Romanticism and the Maritime Empire of Culture.* Charlottesville: University of Virginia Press, 2010.

3 Margaret Cohen, *The Novel and the Sea.* Princeton: Princeton University Press, 2010.

4 Dan Brayton, *Shakespeare's Ocean: An Ecocritical Exploration.* Charlottesville: University of Virginia Press, 2012.

5 Siobhan Carroll, *An Empire of Air and Water: Uncolonizable Spaces in the British Imagination, 1750–1850.* Philadelphia: University of Pennsylvania Press, 2015.

6 Steve Mentz, *Shipwreck Modernity: Ecologies of Globalization, 1550–1719.* Minneapolis: University of Minnesota Press, 2015.

7 Stacy Alaimo, *Exposed: Environmental Politics and Pleasures in Posthuman Times.* Minneapolis: University of Minnesota Press, 2016.

8 Karin Amimoto Ingersoll, *Waves of Knowing: A Seascape Epistemology.* Durham: Duke University Press, 2016.

9 Lowell Duckert, *For All Waters: Finding Ourselves in Early Modern Waterscapes.* Minneapolis: University of Minnesota Press, 2017.

10 Astrida Neimanis, *Bodies of Water: Posthuman Feminist Phenomenology.* London: Bloomsbury, 2017.

The remainder of this bibliographic essay provides full citations to the materials quoted in *Ocean*.

The book's epigraphs comes from Rachel Carson, *Under the Sea-Wind* (New York: Penguin, 1996) 3 and Herman Melville, *Moby-Dick*, Hershel, Parker and Harrison Harford, eds. (New York: Norton, 2002) 40. The preface quotes Gilles Deleuze and Felix Guattari, *A Thousand Plateaus: Capitalism and Schizophrenia*, Brian Massumi, trans. (Minneapolis: University of Minnesota Press, 1987) 508–10.

The first chapter, "Two Origins," quotes Jeffrey Jerome Cohen and Lindy Elkins-Tanton, *Earth* (London: Bloomsbury, 2017) 19; Elaine Morgan, *The Aquatic Ape Hypothesis*, 2nd ed. (London: Souvenir Press, 2017); Melville, *Moby-Dick*, 1.19; Diana Nyad, *Other Shores* (New York: Random House, 1978); Rachel Carson, *The Sea Around Us* (New York: Oxford University Press, 1951) 3, 15; Philip Steinberg, *The Social Construction of the Ocean* (Cambridge: Cambridge University Press, 2001); Édouard Glissant, *Poetics of Relation*, Betsy Wing, trans. (Ann Arbor: University of Michigan Press, 1997) 6.

The second chapter, "Seafood before History," quotes Wallace Nichols, *Blue Mind: The Surprising Science that Shows Being Near, In, On, or Under Water Can Make You Happier, Healthier, More Connected, and Better at What You Do* (New York: Back Bay Books, 2015) 9, 106; John Gillis, *The Human Shore: Seacoasts in History* (Chicago: University of Chicago Press, 2012) 20, 38, 9; Elaine Morgan, *The Aquatic Ape Hypothesis*, 2nd ed. (London: Souvenir Press, 2017); Christopher Connery, "'There was no more sea': The Supersession of the Ocean from the Bible to Hyperspace," *Journal of Historical Geography* 32 (2006) 173–201; Catherine Keller, *The Face of the Deep: A Theology of Becoming* (London: Routledge, 2003); Barry Cunliffe, *Europe Between the Oceans: Themes and Variations,*

9000 BC–AD 1000 (New Haven: Yale University Press, 2008); *The Bible / King James Version* (New York: Penguin, 2006) 779–80; Kimberly Patton, *The Sea Can Wash Away All Evils: Modern Marine Pollution and the Ancient Cathartic Ocean* (New York: Columbia University Press, 2008) 10, 132, 122; Carl Safina, "Toward a Sea Ethic," *The American Prospect*, November 2008, https://prospect.org /article/toward-sea-ethic, accessed March 2019; Amitav Ghosh, *The Great Derangement: Climate Change and the Unthinkable* (Chicago: University of Chicago Press, 2017); Carl Schmitt, *Land and Sea: A World-Historical Meditation*, Samuel Garrett Zeitlin, trans. (Candor, NY: Telos Books, 2015) 33; Charles Olson, *Call Me Ishmael: A Study of Melville* (New York: Globe, 1947) 118, 117; Gaston Bachelard, *Water and Dreams: An Essay on the Imagination of Water*, Edith R. Farrell, trans. (Dallas: Pegasus Foundation, 1983) 31.

The third chapter, "Myth I: Odysseus," quotes Michel Serres, *The Natural Contract*, Elizabeth MacArthur and William Paulson, trans. (Ann Arbor: University of Michigan Press, 1995); the *Iliad* from Christopher Logue, *War Music: An Account of Homer's Iliad* (New York: FSG, 2015) 319, 322; Shakespeare, *Macbeth,* Samuel Clark and Pamela Mason, eds. (London: Bloomsbury, 2015) 2.2.63; Homer, *The Odyssey*, Emily Wilson, trans. (New York: Norton, 2018) 5.151–3, 156–8, 5.224, 5.344–5, 5.301, 5.340, 5.362, 5.373–5, 5.451–5, 5.477, 5.492–3; Northrop Frye, *A Natural Perspective: The Development of Shakespearean Comedy and Romance* (New York: Columbia University Press, 1965) 1–2.

The fourth chapter, "Wet Globalization I," quotes Simon L. Lewis and Mark A. Maslin, *The Human Planet: How We Created the Anthropocene,*(New Haven: Yale University Press, 2018) 166, 318, 156, 158, 13; Alfred Crosby, *The Columbian Exchange: Biological and Cultural Consequences of 1492,* 30th anniversary ed. (Santa

Barbara: Praeger, 2003) 3; Charles C. Mann, *1491: New Revelations of the Americas before Columbus* (New York: Vintage, 2005); Charles C. Mann, *1493: Uncovering the New World Columbus Created* (New York: Vintage, 2001) xxiv; Jason W. Moore, *Capitalism in the Web of Life: Ecology and the Accumulation of Capital* (London: Verso, 2015) 3, 78; J. H. Parry, *The Discovery of the Sea* (Berkeley: University of California Press, 1974); David Wallace-Wells, *The Uninhabitable Earth: Life After Warming,* (New York: Tim Duggan Books, 2019); Olaudah Equiano, *The Interesting Narrative and Other Writings*, Vincent Carretta, ed. (New York: Penguin, 2003) 55; Édouard Glissant, *Poetics of Relation*, Betsy Wing, trans. (Ann Arbor: University of Michigan Press, 1997) 6; Marcus Rediker, *The Slave Ship: A Human History* (New York: Viking, 2007) 348, 354; Derek Walcott, "The Sea is History," in *Selected Poems,* Edward Baugh, ed. (New York: FSG, 2007) 137–9; Fred D'Aguiar, *Feeding the Ghosts* (New York: Ecco, 1999) 3; Edmund Morgan, *American Slavery, American Freedom: The Ordeal of Colonial Virginia* (New York: Norton, 1975); Richard Price, *Travels with Tooy: History, Memory, and the African-American Imagination* (Chicago: University of Chicago Press, 2007); Neil Roberts, *Freedom as Marronage* (Chicago: University of Chicago Press, 2015) 9, 174, 33. I introduced the phrase "wet globalization" in *Shipwreck Modernity: Ecologies of Globalization, 1550–1719* (Minneapolis: University of Minnesota Press, 2015). Vincent Carretta's groundbreaking research on Equiano has suggested that he may have been born in the Carolinas, in which case his account of the Middle Passage would be a powerful fiction, rather than pure autobiography.

The fifth chapter, "Sea Poetry I," quotes Barry Cunliffe, *Europe Between the Oceans: Themes and Variations, 9000 BC–AD 1000* (New Haven: Yale University Press, 2008); Josiah Blackmore,

Manifest Perdition: Shipwreck Narrative and the Disruption of Empire (Minneapolis: University of Minnesota Press, 2002) xix, 26, 22; Luís Vaz de Camões, *The Lusiads,* Landeg White, trans. (Oxford: Oxford University Press, 1997), 5.39.1, 5.38.1–4, 5.39.3–8, 5.38.7, 5.42.1–2, 5–6, 5.43.3, 5.14.5, 5.44.6–7, 5.55.3–8, 5.56.3, 5.59.5–8, 4.102.1–2, 4.104.8; David Quint, *Epic and Empire: Politics and Generic Form from Virgil to Milton* (Princeton: Princeton University Press, 1993) 99–130; John Masefield, "Sea Fever," *Sea Fever: Selected Poems of John Masefield*, Philip Errington, ed. (Manchester: Carcanet Press, 2005) 10; Plato, *The Dialogues of Plato: Laws,* Benjamin Jowett, trans. (Oxford: Oxford University Press, 1892) lxvii; Margaret Cohen, *The Novel and the Sea,* (Princeton: Princeton University Press, 2010) 42; Hesiod, *Works and Days*, Gregory Nagy, trans. (Center for Hellenic Studies, Harvard University: https://chs.harvard.edu/CHS/article/display/5290, accessed March 2019).

The sixth chapter, "Sailors," quotes Donna Haraway, "A Cyborg Manifesto," *Manifestly Haraway*, Cary Wolfe, ed. (Minneapolis: University of Minnesota Press, 2016) 5, 6, 9, 52, 55, 57, 68; Joseph Conrad, *Lord Jim,* Cedric Watts and Robert Hampson, eds. (New York: Penguin, 1986) 100; Smith's *Sea Grammar* quoted in Margaret Cohen, *Novel and the* Sea, (Princeton: Princeton University Press, 2010) 42; Marcus Rediker, *Villains of All Nations: Atlantic Pirates in the Golden Age* (Boston: Beacon Press, 2005); I. C. Campbell, "The Lateen Sail in World History," *Journal of World History* 6:1 (Spring 1995) 1–23; Stan Ulanksi, *The Gulf Stream: Tiny Plankton, Giant Bluefin, and the Amazing Story of the Powerful River in the Atlantic* (Chapel Hill: University of North Carolina Press, 2008); Joseph Conrad, *The Mirror of the Sea* (Marlboro: The Marlboro Press, 1988) 26.

The seventh chapter, "Interlude," relies on Marc Levinson, *The Box: How the Shipping Container Made the World Smaller and the*

World Economy Bigger, 2nd ed. (Princeton: Princeton University Press, 2016). The chapter quotes Federico García Lorca, *Poet in New York* (Penguin: New York, 2002) 63, 69, 157; Kurt Schlichting, *Waterfront Manhattan: From Henry Hudson to the High Line* (Baltimore, Johns Hopkins University Press, 2018) 179; "The Forgotten Space," dir. Allan Sekula and Noël Burch (2010); Allan Sekula, *Fish Story* (Düsseldorf: Richter Verlag, 1995) 106; Robert Sullivan, *The Meadowlands: Wilderness Adventures at the Edge of a City* (New York: Scribner, 1998) 15, 61.

The eighth chapter, "Sea Poetry II," quotes Byron and Walt Whitman from Jonathan Raban's *The Oxford Book of the Sea* (Oxford: Oxford University Press, 1992) 179, 254. I paraphrase the argument of W. H. Auden, *The Enchafèd Flood, or The Romantic Iconography of the Sea* (London: Faber and Faber, 1950). I quote Emily Dickinson from Ralph W. Franklin's *The Poems of Emily Dickinson* (Cambridge: Harvard University Press, 1999): 931 ("An Everywhere of Silver"); 314 ("'Hope' is the thing with feathers"); 359 ("A Bird, came down the walk"); 857 ("She rose to His requirement"); 800 ("I never saw a Moor"); 269 ("Wild nights"); 219 ("My River runs to Thee"); 227 ("Two swimmers wrestled on the spar"); 656 ("I started Early— Took my Dog—"); 706 ("I cannot live with you"); 387 ("The Moon is distant from the Sea"); 206 ("Least Rivers"); 377 ("At least—to pray—is left"); 746 ("It tossed—and tossed"); 143 ("Exultation is the going"); 1286 ("There is no Frigate like a Book"); 737 ("I many times thought Peace had come"); 33 ("Whether my bark went down at sea"). I also cite *Macbeth* 1.2.28–9.

The ninth chapter, "Myth II," quotes Keats and Tennyson from Jonathan Raban, *Oxford Book of the Sea* (Oxford: Oxford University Press, 2000) 183, 264; William Diaper's *Nereides, or Sea-Eclogues* (London: E. Sanger, 1712) from Steve Mentz, *Shipwreck Modernity:*

Ecologies of Globalization, 1550-1719 (Minneapolis: University of Minnesota Press, 2015) 143; Hans Christian Andersen's *The Little Mermaid* (1837) (from SurLaLune's online edition, http://www.surl alunefairytales.com/littlemermaid/, accessed March 2019); and Herman Melville, *Moby-Dick*, 2nd ed., Hershel Parker and Harrison Hayford, eds.(New York: Norton, 2002): 10.56, 10.55, 3.36, 4.38, 3.56, 110.363–7, 72.255, 4.36, 12.59, 111.367. I also refer to my earlier thoughts on Queequeg from *At the Bottom of Shakespeare's Ocean* (London: Bloomsbury, 2009) 44–7.

The tenth chapter, "Wet Globalization II," quotes Peter Sloterdijk's *Spheres* trilogy in English translation: *Bubbles*, Wieland Hoban, trans. (Los Angeles: semiotext(e), 2011) 20, 64, 60; *Globes*, Wieland Hoban, trans. (Los Angeles: semiotext(e), 2014); *Foams*, Wieland Hoban, trans. (Los Angeles: semiotext(e), 2016); Margaret Cohen, *The Novel and the Sea* (Princeton: Princeton University Press, 2010), 201–13; Joseph Conrad, *Mirror of the Sea* (Marlboro: The Marlboro Press, 1988) 24, 121, 20, 63, 78, 32; Olaudah Equiano, *The Interesting Narrative and Other Writings*, Vincent Carretta, ed. (New York: Penguin, 2003) 58; Édouard Glissant, *Poetics of Relation*, Betsy Wing, trans. (Ann Arbor: University of Michigan Press, 1997) 5; Stephanie Smallwood, *Saltwater Slavery: A Middle Passage from African to American Diaspora* (Cambridge: Harvard University Press, 2007) 13; Marcus Rediker, *The Slave Ship: A Human History* (New York: Viking, 2007) 10; Neil Roberts, *Freedom as Marronage* (Chicago: University of Chicago Press, 2015) , 11, 15, 181. I also refer to the Transatlantic Slave Trade Database, maintained by Harvard University's Hutchins Center for African and African American Research, https://hutchinscenter.fas.harvard.edu/trans-atlantic-s lave-trade-database, accessed March 2019. Information about the Dzieci Theatre group, who performed *Makbet* in the shipping container and subsequently in my container-shaped classroom, can be found at http://dziecitheatre.org/, accessed March 2019.

The eleventh chapter, "Blue Environmentalism," quotes all four of Rachel Carson's full-length books, *Under the Sea-Wind*, Linda Lear, intr., Howard Frech, ills. (New York: Penguin, 1996) 65, 3, 106, 162, 162; *The Sea Around Us*, Ann Zwinger intr., Jeffrey Levinton, aft. (Oxford: Oxford University Press, 1989) 3, 7, 75, 76, 97; *The Edge of the Sea*, Sue Hubbell, intr. (Boston: Houghton Mifflin, 1998) 1150, 250; and *Silent Spring*, 50th anniversary ed. (Boston: Houghton Mifflin, 2002) 1, 150–1. I also quote Aldo Leopold, *A Sand County Almanac*, 2nd ed. (Oxford: Oxford University Press, 1968) 204, 129, 203; Catriona Sandilands, "Unnatural Passions?: Notes Toward a Queer Ecology," *Invisible Cultures* (2005), http://www.rochester.edu/in_visible_culture/Issue_9/sandilands.html, accessed March 2019; Jeffrey Jerome Cohen, *Stone: An Inhuman Ecology* (Minneapolis: University of Minnesota Press, 2015); and Emily Wilson's translation of Homer, *The Odyssey*, (New York: W. W. Norton, 2018) 22.468–74.

The twelfth chapter, "Swimmers," quotes Charles Sprawson, *The Haunts of the Black Masseur: The Swimmer as Hero* (Minneapolis: University of Minnesota Press, 2000) 13, 9, 17, 91, 176, 190; Astrida Neimanis, *Bodies of Water: Posthuman Feminist Phenomenology* (London: Bloomsbury, 2017) 26; Leanne Shapton, *Swimming Studies* (New York: Blue Rider Press/Penguin, 2012) 195; James Hamilton-Paterson, *Seven Tenths: The Sea and Its Thresholds* (New York: Europa Editions, 2009) 332, 289; and *Playing with Water* (New York: New Amsterdam Press, 1987) 8; Nicholas Orme, *Early British Swimming, 55 BC—AD 1719* (Exeter: University of Exeter Press, 1983); Alain Corbin, *The Lure of the Sea: The Discovery of the Seaside in the Western World, 1740–1850,* Jocelyn Phelps, trans. (New York:

Penguin, 1995) 69. Quotations from Christopher Middleton's 1595 translation of Everard Digby's *De Arte Natandi* (1587) come from Orme's edition: 115, 117, 119, 150, 164, 134. I quote Vanessa Daws' art-book, *Psychoswimography: Santa Barbara* (Dublin, 2014, self-published). I refer to Samuel de Champlain's *Treatise of Seamanship* (1632) and Fredric Jameson's *A Singular Modernity: Essay on the Ontology of the Present* (London: Verso, 2013). I draw partly on my web essay "Swimming Lessons," in *Hypocrite Reader* 61 (February 2016), http://www.hypocritereader.com/61/swimming-lessons, accessed March 2019. A fuller account of the bodysurfing episode will appear as "Experience is Better than Knowledge: Premodern Ocean Science and the Blue Humanities" in a forthcoming issue of *Configurations*, guest-edited by Stacy Alaimo.

INDEX